Would YOU
MARRY
A FARMER?

Lorna Sixsmith

Write On Track Press
Would You Marry A Farmer?
Lorna Sixsmith

Published in Ireland by Write on Track
ISBN: 978-0-9927632-4-4

To Brian, Will & Kate

Preface

I was reared on a dairy farm and as a child, one of my favourite jobs was bringing in the cows to be milked. When I left home to go to college and then over to England, I never imagined I would be back farming in Garrendenny some years later – back with my husband Brian and two children Kate and Will. I have had a few different roles over the years – secretary, teacher, lecturer, interior designer, farmer, wife, mother, blogger, social media trainer and now a writer. I feel I am somewhat of a fair weather farmer and when I started my blog about the farm, I decided to call it 'Irish Farmerette' to symbolise my "fair-weatheredness".

This book "Would You Marry A Farmer?" was inspired by a blog post entitled "Advice to those considering marrying a farmer" I wrote in September 2012. Demonstrating the truth of what is most farmers' wives lot whereby she can never stand in the right place when working with cattle or sheep (in her husband's opinion), is expected to be telepathic, a good cook, a patient wife, a chauffeur and much more. As it grew in popularity and farmers and non-farmers enjoyed it, the idea formed for a book – to write about what it is like being married to a farmer and it grew from there.

After attending talks on self-publishing and crowdfunding at a social media conference in Wales, the seed for self-publishing was formed. When the blog post received over 50,000 views and 8,000 facebook shares the following week, it seemed like all my planets were lining up in a row for a reason. Crowdfunding would hopefully secure some pre-orders which would partially fund the cost of self-publishing but more importantly, it would reassure me that some people were interested in my book and it would also raise its profile. I tend to be rather impulsive and decided to continue with the writing of the book and run a crowdfunding campaign to determine the interest in such a book. Would people be interested in reading a realistic yet humourous take on being married to a farmer? The answer was yes when 191 people pledged and the deadline was set. All I had to do was finish writing the book, launch a new business **We Teach Social** and co-organise a blog awards – all in four months. Piece of cake for any farmer's wife – right!

Brian and I met in 1987 and started going out together a year later. We moved to England in 1990 and got married in 1992. While living in Bristol and Salisbury, Brian worked as a scientist and completed his MSc and PhD. I went back to university for a BA Hons in English and History and a MA in Irish Studies. After completing a secondary school teaching qualification (PGCE), I taught English and Media Studies for four years.

We moved back to Ireland on 15th July 2002 with our three week old son Will to take over the farm at Garrendenny.

We have been fairly busy since we returned. Our daughter Kate was born in 2004. We built a bungalow for my parents and we moved into the farmhouse in May 2005. We purchased 25 acres five miles away in 2004. In 2007, we purchased 64 acres adjoining our home farm. We are working all hours to pay for it all!

I started blogging in 2008 for my new interior design business. Within a month, Maria Moynihan had discovered my blog, and my business was featured in *Irish Country Living*. From then on, I was hooked on blogging and social media.

Would you Marry a Farmer?

Between changes in the economy and my realisation that social media was my favourite part of the business, I set up **Write on Track** in 2010, followed by **We Teach Social** in 2013 and continued blogging on my personal blog **Irish Farmerette**.

To all farmers, farmerettes and farmhers, I salute you. To all wives, girlfriends, husbands and boyfriends of farmers – I hope you enjoy reading "Would You Marry A Farmer".

Lorna Sixsmith
Garrendenny, Crettyard, Carlow
November 2013

Female Farmers

12.4% of registered farmers in Ireland are female. It is higher in America, Australia and Britain. For the purposes of this book, it presumes that the farmer is male and the intended partner is female. That is not to ignore the number of same sex relationships in rural Ireland.

Women have always been the backbone of Irish farms, the invisible work force and many kept family farms going through good times and bad. It is hoped that the number of registered female farmers will increase as attitudes to succession changes in farming families.

Farmer: noun (non gender specific) - a person who owns or manages a farm.

Farmwife - the wife of a farmer

Farmeress - a woman farmer or the wife of a farmer

Farmerette - a girl or woman who works on a farm (was mentioned in *Finnegan's Wake*)

FarmHer - a new term coined by Americans wishing to emphasise the number of women involved in farming.

RancHer – Canadians capitalise the H to emphasise the number of women involved in ranching.

Contents

The Irish Farmer

What would your ideal farmer be?

Tall, good-looking Farmer, 32, owns 400 acres, 200 cows, dairy and tillage, good road frontage, 2000 sq foot house in showroom condition, large garden, country kitchen with Aga. 5 miles from major town with good nightlife. In possession of a jeep, horsebox and room for a pony. Enjoys hunting. Lives alone, Daily maid. Midlands. Would like to meet a lady to share it with and live happily ever after.

Would you marry him????

OR

Farmer, 38, 82 acres owned, 40 acres rented. 50 cows, 3 donkeys, one bull, 6 pigs, 2 goats, 2 dogs and 3 goldfish. 3 miles from main road. Old farmhouse with character and great potential. Lives with Mammy. Two clapped out tractors, a MF 290 and a John Deere. Enjoys going to the mart. Needs a wife to milk the cows.

Would you marry him????

Section 1

Are Farmers A Good Catch?

The Anglo Celt 25th February 1970

Deasy Fan is a 21 year old Limerick man who would like to get in touch with nice slim farmers' daughters (not those wearing glasses) who are well-off and have good family backgrounds. They must also have their own cars and good jobs. Replies preferred from West Limerick.

Ireland & Her Farmers

Ireland has always been an agricultural nation. Most Irish people are only one or two generations removed from farming. Many city dwellers have memories of visiting grandparents or other relatives on their farm. They remember feeding calves, hand milking cows or goats, travelling in transport boxes, moving cattle along the road, bringing calves to the mart, picking blackberries along hedgerows, loading small square bales of hay and probably many escapades in between.

Our beautiful landscape is largely created and maintained by farmers. Driving around any part of Ireland, you can see beautiful fields of various shades of greens and yellows, their tones defined by the growth and consumption of grass and the harvesting of silage and corn. Irish fields are very varied in size and shape. Very few are regular rectangular shapes, which makes the view all the more charming and interesting. Separated from each other by stone walls, fences or dense hedging and trees which offer shelter from sun, wind and rain, all are picturesque. Dotted with cattle and sheep or boasting a fine crop of corn or rapeseed, some fields will have tractors driving up and down as they spread slurry, plough furrows or cut silage. Ireland's roads are edged with hedging backing onto farmlands, hedging that is kept trimmed and in shape by Ireland's farmers.

Let us not mention the pungent smell of slurry that wafts around the countryside after the sweet smelling grass has been harvested for silage or the muck that sometimes falls onto the roads behind the farmyard manure spreader. Neither will we dwell on the traffic queues that form on country roads when a farmer is driving slowly with his tractor and trailer or moving cattle and sheep. Let us concentrate instead on the beautiful varied landscape of the Emerald Isle and how much of it is due to the diverse nature of Irish farms and the hard work of Irish farmers.

Ireland is called the Emerald Isle for a very good reason. The amount of rain that falls makes the landscape very green all year round. It gets the prevailing winds from the Atlantic Ocean. The clouds see land and decide to unload themselves. Therefore the West receives more rain than the East. Never travel to the west without a raincoat or an umbrella, essential pieces of equipment. The weather is usually mild, often with a grey sky and a mist that is down for the day. "A grand soft day" is so named because the drops of rain are relatively gentle and will not wash away seed, crops or fertiliser.

Should Ireland ever be without rain for a fortnight, the usually mucky cow paths around farms turn to dust and wellington boots can be replaced by old shoes for a little while. Farms with wet land enjoy the fact that the existing moisture in the earth, when combined with the heat, sends grass growing at extraordinary speed. Farmers of dry land start to hope for rain while everyone else berates them for it.

The Irish farmer has a passion for his land like no other. Most farmers hold onto their land as fiercely as if it is their only child. Only when a farmer is in a box and pushing up daisies does he really cease to be a farmer. Each field is named and it is not just for convenience. They are called after their shape, size or position. Some fields are named after landmarks such as ringforts or quarries. Others might be named after tenant farmers now long gone. Giving them names gives them personalities and tightens the bond. Some are firm favourites, perhaps because of their position and view or because the cows always milk well on the grass eaten there. The fields on our farm are called the Big Field, The Chapel Field, Peters, Top Field, The Banks, High Shores, Low Shores, The Lawn, Top of the Lawn, The Letterbox, Top of the Letterbox, Taylors, The Lee, The Bog, Berrygins, Delaneys, Lynups Hill, Wades, Burkes, Bakers Hill, The Hall Field, Malántha, and the Quarry Field. Lynups Hill is my own personal favourite – the wind that blows at the top of the hill is always invigorating and the views are beautiful. The farmer's favourite is High Shores because it is the driest field on the farm, grows the most grass and the cows always milk well from it.

Land only changes hands once every four hundred years in Ireland. Rather than sell the home farm and buy a larger farm elsewhere if trying to expand, farmers purchase land within a comfortable tractor drive. Hence, fragmented farms are very much the norm in Ireland. The farmer has to drive to other parts of the farm daily, jaunting along in his tractor with his dog or helpers safely ensconced within.

The play *The Field* by JB Keane (and subsequent film) demonstrates the ferocious pride that farmers have in their land and their desperation to hold onto it.[1] As The Bull (main character in the play) went to terrible measures to buy the field he had rented, fertilised and cleared of stones, one is reminded the news story which inspired this play was an alleged murder over land.[2] There have been more deaths and feuds over land than one might ever imagine, which of course demonstrates the passion the average farmer has for his territory.

Farms are not necessarily an asset to be disposed of and sold. While they are worth a bob or two, most farmers would have serious regrets if they had to sell their farm. They see themselves as custodians of their farms; they are there to nurture it, to see it yield its best produce, to dig it and till it and grow grass or wheat, not just for their own income but so it can be passed on to the next generation and the next.

Irish Farmers

Apart from being tied to the land almost as if with an umbilical cord, what is the Irish farmer really like? Is the Irish farmer the stereotypical male farmer who spends much of his time at the mart and in the pub? Does he work all hours of the day and night? Is he too mean to get married? Are the farmers lazy and controlling, holding onto the cheque book while their wives and workmen do most of the labour? Are they the beggars of Europe, with a cap in their large gnarled hands, looking to Brussels for their single farm payment handouts to be dropped into the begging cup for another year of "set-aside" and wildlife areas? Is the Irish farmer a "good catch", a "fine thing", a good looking, fit and muscular farmer who is an excellent family man and puts his wife and children first?

Irish farmers 1820-1965

A century ago, the "strong farmers" were those who farmed more than thirty acres. They were amongst the most prosperous and were able to employ labourers full-time and seasonally. They may have been seen as a good catch with their large farmhouses, sizeable farm and plenty of workers, but if you wanted to marry one of them, you would have needed to come from a comparable farm and bring a sizeable dowry with you. The dowry (gift to his family) would have been a significant amount of money or livestock. You would have been expected to work hard to make the farm a success and rear a family in the large rambling farmhouse. It would have been shared with his parents, or almost certainly his mother, for many years. The house would have boasted a parlour to entertain the priest and other important visitors. He was probably an eldest son if he was inheriting; younger brothers often became doctors, lawyers or priests. If there were sufficient funds, a second farm might have been purchased for the second son. If you were a "strong farmer's daughter", you may have served your time in a shop or trained as a nurse or teacher before you married a farmer, bringing your dowry with you. Your other alternatives would have been entering a convent (which also required a dowry), emigrating or remaining single and looking after your aged parents.

Most Irish farms were less than thirty acres back then. If a farmer owned between five and thirty acres he was considered reasonably well off. Most farms had a number of different enterprises, known as mixed farming. Even if a farm was predominantly a dairy farm, there were poultry for eggs and meat, a couple of pigs, some sheep or goats and crops such as corn and beet. Farmers' wives worked alongside them milking cows and churning butter. Dwellings would have varied from thatched cottages to two-storey farmhouses.

Cottiers rented half an acre from a larger farm, using the half acre for their dwelling and to produce food. They worked on neighbouring farms at busy times, offsetting wages against the rent. Living in a one roomed hut (often without a window), life must have been pretty bleak, yet they had their own supply of food for most of the year, even if it was an unvaried diet of potatoes supplied from the land they rented. They would not have been able to afford a cow but many kept a pig, hens and perhaps a goat for milk and meat. The pig was usually sold to contribute to the rent. The Potato Famine of 1845-51 put an end to this system of living for many people but some cottiers and small farmers still travelled abroad looking for work, going to Scotland or England during the harvest time.

Being married to one of these men did not mean an easy life as the farm had to be maintained while he was away. Tasks included manuring the ground; harvesting oats, hay and turnips for winter fodder; and milking the single cow. Most work had to be done with hand implements such as spades and scythes. Calluses on your hands would probably have been the least of your problems if you had married one of these men. With the arrival of the milkman to a western area in 1961, a number of wives decided to sell their cows and buy their milk instead. Although it caused consternation amongst their elders and neighbours, the women found the supply of milk changed their lives and meant that they only had to tend to a vegetable plot to provide food for their own table. It was claimed that the milkman did more for these women's lives than the installation of electricity and that is saying a lot! The women who had got rid of the cows looked younger, were less weather-beaten and had fewer wrinkles. They had time to take more pride in their appearance and enjoy some leisure.[3]

The number of farmers in Ireland has been decreasing year on year. Many older farmers do not have successors and the farms are sold when they retire or die. It has become more difficult for those owning small farms to eke out a livelihood. Hence, the farm is not going to provide a sustainable income for any of their children. Whether the system of farming is dairy, beef, sheep or tillage, it either needs to be of sufficient size to support a family or it will require a second income nowadays. Many part-time farmers turned to building work during the Celtic Tiger years to supplement their farming income considerably. [4] Those jobs are now gone and their overall income is down. Farming practices are changing on many farms as a result.

Gendered nature of farming

The majority of Irish farmers are male. Only 12.4% of registered farmers (those with land and a herd number) are female. Yet, on almost every farm where there is a woman, she is involved in the farm to some extent. Some women farm full-time alongside the male farmer either as his wife, mother, sister or daughter but most do not describe themselves as farmers and are not recognised as such. Many women are the head bottle washers, administrators, book-keepers, cooks, head gardeners, managing directors of housekeeping, key organisers, taxi drivers, purchasing managers, sales directors, key negotiators, and more. Those who are not active on the farm on a daily basis are almost certainly the chief assistants at busy times such as calving, lambing and harvesting. They feed contractors and helpers and bring tea to the men in the field. Every farm wife stands in a gap sooner or later. [5] Yet women have largely been invisible in farming up until now. Their contributions were not recognised by farmers or by the industry.

During the National Farmers' Association campaign for Farmers' Rights of 1966-67, when farmers marched to Dublin, protested outside the Department of Agriculture for twenty one days and nights, were imprisoned, and negotiated with the Taoiseach, the farm wives fed them as they progressed towards Dublin. It was the farm wives that kept the farms going and took the farmers places in the protest while they attended meetings. It was farm women who drove tractors through Dublin in March 1967, who marched to Portlaoise prison and to Dublin. It was presumed by the farmers that their wives would support them and keep the home fires burning. The women assumed it too and many did not notice that their role was invisible, just as it had been for many decades.[6]

My maternal grandmother had a busy poultry business in addition to helping on the farm and rearing eight children, yet it was not viewed as "real farm work" but as pin money. She was a savvy business woman, she employed a woman on a part-time basis and she was an incredibly hard worker. Women were (and still are) the backbone to many farms and kept them going through good times and bad.

Many farming activities are still divided according to gender. If you visit the mart on a busy day, most of the people there are men, standing around catching up on the latest news and musing over the changes in cattle or sheep prices since the previous week. If you go to an Irish Farmers' Association meeting, most of the attendees are male. Many women say they feel out of place, uncomfortable and slightly intimidated at such occasions. The IFA National Farm Family committee was set up to recognise the role of women in farming and to increase women's involvement in the IFA. If you were to call into an Irish Countrywomen's Association meeting, every person there will be female and likely to be of a certain vintage. According to Gibbons, the ICA was a feminist movement when it was set up in 1910 as it provided a way for women to unite. As long as they did not openly question or challenge the status quo, they could work for women's interests.[7] Each guild has individual differences depending on the interests of those in the group. Some provide lessons in crafting, flower arranging and cooking. As crafting makes a comeback and the ICA grows to 11,000 members, I remind myself I must go along to a knitting class. My farmer believes some cooking tips might help me to become a perfect farming wife!

Farming in the public sphere in Ireland still tends to be somewhat gendered, with the men taking the traditionally masculine role of selling and buying (at the mart) and decision making (at IFA meetings) whereas in many cases, women are continuing in the traditionally feminine role of nurturing, mothering and domesticity. However, the outlook is changing. Women and Agriculture conferences play a wonderful role in bringing farm women together and are now focusing on the role women play in the future of farming apart from the traditional roles of farm wife as book-keeper, cook and chief assistant.

While many farmers see farming as the only occupation they would ever like to do, "tis in the blood ... I can't explain it. I suppose I love what I do"[8], roles in family farms are changing. As is evident from Caitriona Ní Laoire's research, farmers saw themselves as landowners and father figures while the feminine roles of domesticity and nurturing were carried out by farm wives. In recent years, as more women are working outside the home on a full-time or part-time basis (remember it is only forty years since the marriage bar was lifted[9]), the male farmer is now playing a much bigger role in childcare. Many part-time farmers worked off farm during the building boom of the Celtic Tiger. They are now farming full-time and they are the ones collecting the children from school, doing homework with them and cooking dinner. They are learning what it means to multi-task and embracing their feminine side. The household chores are shared and this can only be positive for children to see that the roles can be shared rather than strictly gendered. I can remember being surprised seeing a friend's father cooking a meal and I am sure I wasn't the only farmer's child to presume that men could not cook.

Macra na Feirme offers a social outlet to young farmers of both sexes.[10] Men and women have fun together through pursuits such as walking holidays, public debating and dancing, and equality seems to be more on the cards. More females are following careers in veterinary medicine and in agricultural sciences now. Previously, most farmers only considered a son as their successor and many older farmers would still sell a farm or rent it out rather than let a daughter take over. How farmers make their decisions regarding their successor in the future will determine changes in the traditionally gendered nature of Irish farming.

What Are Irish Farmers Really Like?

If you are looking for a rich farmer, you are likely to be disappointed, since they are as hard to find as needles in a haystack. As claimed by Ni Laoire[11], many farmers are not motivated by profit, even now. Yes, they want an income to put bread on the table, to educate their children, to have a car and a tractor, to invest money back into the farm, to "do up" the farmhouse perhaps, but most farmers are not motivated by money alone. They take pride in seeing their animals and crops do well. They are optimists by nature and if their income is down due to low prices or bad weather, they will hope for a better year the following year. Their participation in discussion groups highlights where expenses can be reduced and how income can be increased. However,

Mother Nature also plays a huge part when much of a farm's profitability comes from keeping animals out at grass for as many days in the year as possible. Even if a farmer has a good year, he is unlikely to retire early or go on two foreign holidays every year. Farmers are more likely to invest in new machinery or more land if they are doing well. If you would prefer a new kitchen, expensive shoes or the latest designer handbag from the extra profits, you will have to be a skilled negotiator.

Many farmers are happy to be working long hours, albeit in relatively harsh conditions, as long as they are out of doors and their own boss. Some tend to look with disdain at those who opt for an "easier" office job, an occupation that is indoors and has the security of a monthly salary and a pension. It is the farmers who are the tough cookies. Good farmers have to be good business people, able to weigh up their options and think outside the box. Some decisions taken will not pay dividends – perhaps because of poor foresight, perhaps because of inadequate planning, but it can often be down to unexpected bad weather or unforeseen changes in the economy.

Farmers tend to be optimistic and flexible – they have to be in order to enjoy the occupation and do it year after year. They will put their life's work, heart and soul into their farm. Even when they retire, most farmers will wish to continue to know what is going on, to help out with some jobs and to see their grandchildren out feeding calves and helping to herd. My father continues to wash out the milking parlour, helps with bedding and feeding of calves and assists when moving cattle and with dosing. He is never happier than when he is out and about, seeing grass growing, cows milking and fine cattle going to the factory.

However, farming has become increasingly isolated. From having labour units or neighbours helping each other at busy times, when there would be chat and laughter and gossip, now a farmer might not see anyone except his immediate family from day to day. If he has a fragmented farm he may see other farmers on the road while travelling, but his only other company might be delivery men, sales representatives from agricultural companies or his beloved dog. For farmers who are unmarried and do not have any family members living nearby to chat, the isolation can cause pressures such as bad weather or financial concerns to intensify. Many farmers are happy in their own company but for those who prefer interaction with others, farming can be a lonely occupation.

Would You Have Married A Farmer In 1950?

There were many single farmers in Ireland in the mid 20th century and they were not necessarily viewed as eligible bachelors. Many farmers' sons waited until they were in their forties and fifties before they married, if they married at all. One third of all men over 55 in Ireland were unmarried during the 1950s.

The eldest son usually inherited the farm and looked after his parents while younger siblings emigrated. By the time the farmers got their chance to marry, their potential brides had wedded someone else or had emigrated. While a minority succeeded in finding a wife, many of the bachelor farmers faced a lonely future with no successor to their farm.

Why did farmers leave it so late to marry?

Many farming sons were living isolated lives with elderly parents. Many were treated as young boys and had to ask for the price of a pint even though they were grown men, or received a pittance as payment. Their social skills were limited as was their confidence with the opposite sex. A 27 year old farmer wrote to the Sunday Independent claiming he only received 12.5 shillings per week for his work, he stated he would not be able to marry for at least ten years as his father was only 57. Having left school at fourteen (like his siblings), he felt his options were few and argued that older farmers should be taxed if their sons are unmarried when aged over 25.[12] William Trevor refers to these older bachelors as "mountain men" in *The Ballroom of Romance*. "The middle-aged men ... came down from the hills like mountain goats, released from their mammies and from the smell of animals and soil"[13]. The image wouldn't exactly inspire you to agree to a blind date with one of them, would it?

The patriarchal and parental control of marriage was intense but why did so many obey their parents? Why did they wait so long before getting married? According to Connell, people partly blamed themselves for the deaths resulting from the Famine. They saw the pre-Famine early marriages as being irresponsible and as a society, they were adamant they would not marry until they could afford to support a family. They did not want to risk starvation or forced emigration again if they could prevent it by marrying later.[14] As late marriage became the norm, particularly for men, it was accepted that many bachelors were single until they were in their fifties. Unfortunately, it seems that many regretted it when it was too late.

Some claimed that the high numbers of bachelors and spinsters were due to the influence of the Catholic Church, but it must be remembered that Protestants made up a quarter of the population in the early twentieth century and their marriage patterns were similar. According to Guinnane, many people who did not emigrate were happy to accept that marriage would be late or might not happen. Letters from abroad revealed life in big cities to be uncertain and those living as farmers in Ireland had the security of their land and the kinship of relatives and neighbours.[15] Living as a single farmer was viewed as preferable to uncertainty and emigration and after all, while there was life there was hope of finding a suitable bride.

> ***Freeman's Journal* 25th September 1915**
> **Matrimony – A Farmer,** RC, with means, would like to meet a farmer's daughter or business girl with means for matrimony. Address 8930 Freeman's Office.

As this advertisement shows, there was little impulsiveness regarding marriage. It was a carefully considered financial arrangement and it required an amount of money from both parties. Love and passion came second and third. To marry this farmer, you would have needed a sizeable dowry.

It wasn't just men who were remaining single in large numbers; the rate of marriage for women fell too. Almost a quarter of Irish women aged 45-54 were unmarried in 1926. While some stayed to look after ageing parents and worked with a brother on the farm, others moved away from rural areas, leaving potential husbands behind. Many women migrated from rural areas to towns and then emigrated.[16]

The rate of marriage in Ireland was one of the lowest in the world from 1922–1971.[17]

Although late marriage came to be seen as the norm, lots of people were worried about the large numbers of unmarried farmers during the 1940s and 1950s. Apart from the number of men living in isolation, commentators were concerned about the "cases where young farmers had to wash their own clothes and do their own cooking, while there were many good-looking girls in the neighbourhood who were forced to waste their charms on the desert air."[18] So why didn't these good looking girls want to marry these bachelor farmers who were looking for a wife? Were they not seen as eligible and attractive?

Matchmaking & Dowries

A married woman had superiority over her unmarried sisters and certainly over her unmarried sister-in-law. Getting married was not as easy as it sounds and it was actually quite an achievement. Men who could afford to marry were not that plentiful; women had to have sufficient means to buy their place in the marriage stakes by way of their dowry. Because farming practices had changed somewhat and allegedly women were not contributing to the farm income to the same extent, the dowry became seen as a "fine for the transfer of a redundant dependant female from one family to another".[19] In effect, a woman's father had to compensate her husband for the expense of keeping her after marriage.

Perhaps because of the unavailability of a dowry or because they wanted to secure their own economic independence, many women emigrated. It might be that they emigrated to find a husband, to be able to marry at a younger age than they would in Ireland (and possibly to marry a younger husband too). Judging by the advertisements in the personal columns, very few farmers would have taken a wife without a dowry even though men outnumbered women significantly. As demonstrated by this advertisement in *The Irish Times*, marriageable men needed the dowry to fund the emigration of siblings or their parents' retirement, enable a sister to get married or improve the farm:

The Irish Times 8th June 1875
A Business Man, about 35, wishes to meet a lady of the business or farming class, about the same age, with a view to marriage; she will require to have some means, so the advertiser can make a settlement. Write to Alpha, P412, office of this paper, giving real name in confidence. Letters returned if desired.

The following advertisement in the *Freemans Journal* suggests the farmer was not just looking for a wife – he was also looking for a farm. He was being choosy about location and wanted one close to town too. Presumably this was because he wanted to visit the market and pub easily. Hopefully all women ran a mile and he stayed single!

Freeman's Journal 31st July 1916
Matrimony – Bachelor 42 (RC) with £900 wishes to correspond with R.C. lady, 25-35, with farm adjacent to town, when answering state particulars, age, extent of farm etc, strictly confidential. Address 338 Freeman's Office.

Dowries varied from hard cash to the provision of cows, sheep or household items. According to Willie Daly (an Irish matchmaker), a father felt that "a picture of John F Kennedy and Jacqueline, and a statue of a hen and a clutch of chickens" was a good dowry while another was offering "ten silver sovereigns, a three-legged stool and a fine feather bed"[20]. If the family had relatives working in America, the dowry was usually cash. The money then went into the ownership of her husband, or if the farm hadn't become his yet, it went to his parents. Rather bizarrely, the one payment could make its way around half a dozen families, enabling marriages as one bride funded the marriage of a sister-in-law and so on.[21] The dowry amount for "strong farmers" was substantial and could affect a farmer's own ability to afford a marriage and family if he had to fund a number of sisters. In 1955, a Meath farmer provided each of his six sisters with a dowry of almost £900, much more than the £250 he was obliged to under his father's will.[22] Many parents could only afford a dowry for one or two daughters. If you were a younger sister, your choices might have been limited to entering the convent, emigration or spinsterhood. The decision was probably determined by the person's bravery and ambition, the availability of contacts abroad and the control exerted by her parents. Although the dowry was declining in use by the 1950s and 1960s, if you were a farmer's daughter, your choice of husband would at best have to be approved by your parents and at worst decided by them.

Matchmaking was the method used to arrange marriages between couples from similar backgrounds. Matchmakers were trusted to join people who were likely to be happy together. Key to the success of matchmaking were the negotiations for marriage. The bride's family would examine the quality and size of the potential husband's farm and then negotiate as to the value of her dowry. The number of chains for securing cows in the shed would be checked in case the farmer had temporarily "borrowed" some cows to improve his bargaining position. Marriages weren't necessarily for love and companionship but were often a financial arrangement between two families of similar means. This meant that the class structure of family farms remained unchanged. Marriages were also formed for rather eccentric reasons. A groom's family might have needed a donkey to carry home the turf and remembered a family with a marriageable daughter and a suitable donkey which would serve as the dowry.[23]

The angst in *The Quiet Man* (starring John Wayne and Maureen O'Hara) where a dowry was unpaid was not unknown. Half might have been paid on marriage with a promise to pay the rest at a later date. If that did not happen, sometimes it went to court. A Monaghan mother was sued by her son-in-law in 1933 as she had not paid him £75, the balance of the dowry as agreed in a promissory note. Living on a small farm of six roods, she could not pay it and claimed her son was to have done so.[24]

Many husbands were much older than their wives with a quarter being at least a decade older.[25] It was relatively common for men in their sixties to marry women in their twenties. Willie Daly, recalled one of the first matches he witnessed as a young boy. The prospective bride's aunt and uncle were haggling over her dowry for her marriage to a farmer in his sixties. She was in her late twenties and despite the fact that he was so much older than her, she was happy to be getting married. She would have a home of her own which was particularly welcome as her brother was getting married.[26] Most farms had a single dwelling house and the three generations would live there. If you were a dependant unmarried sister-in-law, you were probably regarded as a burden by your brother's bride and you might not have very much say within the household. You had no home to call your own, no security and little pay. You were probably relatively uneducated, caring for elderly parents, working on the farm and reliant on the kindness of your brother and his wife.

The old man wishing to marry a young woman as in JB Keane's play *Sive* was not that unusual and the story was inspired by a young bride forced to marry a much older man against her will. The prospective bride is eighteen and her family are being paid for the marriage, rather than having to supply a dowry. She is against it and her only way out is suicide on the eve of the wedding. Her future husband is depicted as old, decrepit and lecherous and our sympathy is with the young Sive. Her aunt Mena cannot understand why Sive does not want to marry the old man. Mena married for status and security and sees his land, twenty cows and two servants as impressive. She sees it as a "glass half full" scenario, telling Sive that he will soon die and she will be mistress of her own home. She ignores the evidence that he is lusting after this beautiful teenager and that her upbringing had not prepared her for the harsh reality that made up some women's lives.[27]

There were other reasons why marrying a farmer may not have been number one on a young woman's bucket list. They had to work very hard, usually much harder than their farmer husbands. Studies on family farms during the 1930s showed that the woman would often be up first in the morning. Her jobs included rekindling the fire, preparing breakfast, getting children off to school, making beds, washing up, drawing water, sweeping floors and washing clothing. Her farmwork included milking the cows, making butter, collecting eggs and feeding the various livestock. When it came to mealtimes, there were some parts of the country where the women and children did not sit down to eat until the men had finished. The farm work had to be repeated every evening with the milking of cows and the feeding of calves, chickens and pigs. Turf to be brought in, water collected from the well and bread baked on a griddle.

"Women's work" included the sale of eggs, making butter and milking cows, and many men just did not consider those tasks to be part of their workload.[28] Men collected the monthly milk cheque and the proceeds from the sale of animals and crops. Women's money came from the sale of eggs. In the evenings, the men arrived in from working in the fields and spent their evenings by the fire or at the pub. It was not acceptable for a woman to enter a pub so her life revolved around the home and the farm. When the farm wife did get to sit down by the fire, she was darning or knitting. Add to this the fact that most of them had large families and might be pregnant every couple of years – you can understand why some would run a mile from marriage to a farmer. From the early 1940s on, sympathy was growing for the woman in the home and the difficult conditions under which she had to labour. You will feel tired just reading this account!

> "Nowadays town houses are built for convenience
> and labour saving, for comfort and economy in the
> running of them. The townswoman has a supply of
> running water, a neat range that will not burn much
> fuel and will supply hot water to wash-basin and
> bath in the bathroom and to the wash-up sink in the
> kitchen or scullery. She has hot and cold water, good
> sanitation, electric light, a plug for her electric iron,

cupboard space and plenty of shelves. All this makes heaven for the town home-maker. And all this goes for the plain workman's wife as well as for the doctor's wife in Merrion Square.

The country woman then must drag in the cold water from outside the house. For every basin of hot water she wants, she must lift a heavy kettle on and off the fire. On washing-day, washtubs must be filled and emptied time and again; what it costs in labour to keep her churn and milk vessels clean!

The open fire-place in the country house looks grand and when we think of the lovely cakes that come out of the pot-oven, it makes us quite sentimental - but the truth is that half the heat goes up the chimney with the draught and the old pot-oven is unwieldy and clumsy and out of date.

Now when night falls, the townswoman presses a button and at once there is a light and cheerful glow about her. The countrywoman, like the Wise Virgin in the gospel, has had to clean and tend and fill her lamp before lighting it or else she has to depend on her halfpenny dip. Millions have been spent on the Shannon scheme but it is not the countrywoman who has the benefit of it."

(**Muintir na Tíre Official Handbook, 1941**).

Are Farmers a Good Catch?

The Irish Mammy & Her Bachelor Son

The Irish Mammy was a force to be reckoned with. She thought her son was the best thing ever, unable to do any wrong. She cooked and cleaned for him for years, cooked his favourite dinners, ironed his Sunday shirts to perfection, creased his trousers, polished his shoes, made his bed, picked his dirty socks off the floor and sugared and stirred his tea. She was a wonderfully efficient woman, able to concoct a meal out of a homemade loaf of bread and half a dozen eggs if need be. However, some of them would have bullied their sons too, by maintaining control, deriding their self esteem, discouraging marriage and ensuring they were at their beck and call.

> Poor Paddy Maguire, a fourteen-hour day
> He worked for years. It was he that lit the fire
> And boiled the kettle and gave the cows their hay.
> His mother tall, hard as a Protestant spire,
> Came down the stairs bare-foot at the kettle-call
> And talked to her son sharply: 'Did you let
> The hens out, you?' She had a venomous drawl
> And a wizened face like moth-eaten leatherette.

The Great Hunger – Patrick Kavanagh

No wonder no woman married the fictional Maguire – how could you live with a mother-in-law like that? As demonstrated by Kavanagh, the age difference between marriage partners was often a number of decades, farmers inherited when their father died and their mothers lived for many more years. The presence of a mother-in-law was not necessarily considered an advantage by many prospective brides.

There were situations whereby a mother did not want her son to marry. She did not want her daughter-in-law to become the chief organiser of the home and the mistress of the house. It was a choice between dissuading him from marriage, battling to maintain her seniority with the daughter-in-law or giving in to it. If an Irish farming mammy disapproved of a potential wife, that was often the end of the relationship – it would take a strong man to live with two women at war under the same roof. As a result, many sons were bachelors in their fifties, lonely and living with a widowed mother. Many turned to the pub for solace and companionship. The farm went downhill with increasing debts which resulted in the farm being either inherited by a nephew, sold or claimed by the publican in return for debts owed.

> "The groom's mother might in reality be about to turn into a real demon of a mother-in-law, but even she'd be in good spirits that night because her son had got himself a bride and she could see the possibility of an heir to the throne ... but oftentimes beneath the smiles she would be desperately jealous towards the new wife....The mother-in-law could see that she was about to be left aside, that her position of power was under threat, but she would fight her redundancy very hard and be a very devil. The old saying is that more than one woman in a kitchen is a recipe for disaster."[29]

In *Sive* by JB Keane, the battles between the grandmother Nanna and her daughter-in-law Mena are constant. Mena freely admits that she got married to have a home of her own, to have stability in her life and food on the table. There is little sign of romance between she and her husband and Nanna often pokes fun at her childlessness, something that must have hurt deeply given the importance of children to farming families. Mena ridicules her mother-in-law in return and emphasises her powerlessness in the home, since Mena could have her turned out if she wished.[30]

The tie to the family farm and to one's aged parents is also apparent in William Trevor's short story *The Ballroom of Romance*. Although the weekly dance hall provided opportunities to meet future partners, most women knew that many of the men would never marry "they were wedded already, to stout and whiskey and laziness, to three old mothers somewhere up in the hills." Bowser Egan's excuse to Bridie was that his mother would not permit another woman in the house. Bridie knew he would not marry until his mother was dead.[31] Even though she recognised he was a lazy drunkard, she still opted for an eventual marriage rather than endure a lonely spinsterhood or ridicule at the dance hall. I guess the silver lining was that the dragon of the mother-in-law would be dead!

As emphasised in Kavanagh's *The Great Hunger*, Maguire was "mothered" for too long, he left it too late to marry and now his future is destined to be bleak:

Maguire was faithful to death:
He stayed with his mother till she died
At the age of ninety-one.
She stayed too long,
Wife and mother in one.
When she died
The knuckle-bones were cutting the skin of her son's backside
And he was sixty-five.

Let's face it — bachelor farmers had been spoilt (or controlled) by their mammies for years. It was likely she controlled everything in the house and perhaps made many of the farming decisions too. Once their mother died, these farmers only started to look for a wife when they realised the farm needed a woman and an heir. By the time they discovered no one wanted to marry them, it was too late. Many remained bachelors, with the occasional wealthy farmer able to find a young wife. And so the situation exacerbated, the age difference between wife and husband increasing with each generation[32]. To find a wife who would agree to marry, the farmer often had to have considerable wealth to persuade her, with the help of an able matchmaker.

The Bachelor Farmer in Literature

The portrayal of farmer bachelors in Irish literature wouldn't induce many to consider marriage to them. While many authors might have depicted the gay bachelor life as something to be envied, JB Keane depicted them as rather pitiful, desperate and incredibly lonely in his various plays and epistolary novels, albeit in a way that made the audiences laugh at them.

> "The population of the parish declined with every passing year ..... The truly tragic characters are the middle-aged and more advanced bachelors who walk the land like shadows as if they knew they were the last of their kind. .... they eke out a living from their milch cows and small government supplements. The womenfolk have deserted them for the towns, for the irresistible call of the five day week, the annual

holidays, the modern houses, the urban amenities, and the steady wages."[33]

John Bosco, the main character in *The Chastitute*[34] and *Letters of a Love Hungry Farmer,* hasn't the "makings of a dacent sin in him", and tries to follow the advice of an old friend, a matchmaker, and a young confidante who ends up benefiting from his purse. All he wants is a woman who is reasonably respectable and who would share his life and his bed. He agrees with the matchmaker Mickey when he says "What are we looking for? Isn't it only someone to make our beds and wet our tay and keep us company for the rest of our days with maybe a leg thrown over now and again?" They feel they weren't looking for much and yet still could not find it. The situation was indeed desperate.

Bosco's interludes with various women reveal that they are prostitutes, pregnant or just do not want him. Of the twenty-four eligible women that were once in Tubberbangan, only one married locally. Daughter of a large farmer, she married into a similar sized farm. Twelve emigrated, two became nuns and the rest migrated to the towns where they married shopkeepers, carpenters, doctors and bankers[35]. Bosco and his comrades eventually came to the realisation that any suitable woman had either emigrated or didn't want to marry a farmer.

The priest described the "lonely and typical bachelor farmer as an unshaven lout, fifty-five years old, wearing a long black coat and a cap, ... standing at the door of a public house in Bannabeen with porter stains on his mouth and a bloodstained parcel of boiling beef under his oxter".[36]

He doesn't sound attractive either, does he? The tragedy of the situation is revealed as John Bosco is discovered dead at the end of *Letters of a Love Hungry Farmer.*

Unable to cope with the loneliness anymore, he shoots himself in his own kitchen. In *Letters of a Matchmaker*, the hero concludes with news of his upcoming marriage and the line "A woman is a great thing in a house if 'twas only for wetting the tea you wanted her".[37] Loneliness is seen to be the main difficulty facing rural dwellers, something that could be obliterated by marriage. Could marriage really cure all ills?

Why were farmers not seen as a good catch?

1. If the farmer was young and his father was alive, the bride would have to work even harder and for longer.

2. His mother was probably alive and living in the farmhouse. The relationship might be fraught between the two women.

3. The farmhouse was old and did not have modern conveniences.

4. Many farms were mixed enterprises and much of the farm work was seen as women's work.

5. Women knew they would have to work hard for little reward. Heading to the bright lights and independence of the towns and cities must have seemed much more fun.

6. Equality was rare in a farming relationship. Very few wives had their name on the chequebook. Spending could be significantly curtailed.

7. Some women did not have a dowry so marrying a farmer was not an option. They would not have been accepted by his family.

8. Many potential farming husbands were decades older than their brides.

9. For many, marriage was a financial relationship. Love was a bonus.

Who Did Marry These Farmers?

Some women had to be happy to marry farmers however, otherwise the farmers would have died out without any children to inherit. Although the bachelor farmer was common, the majority did marry. If marriage to a farmer was seen as a hard life, why did some women marry them? Did they marry for love? My grandmothers were both quite young getting married. One was twenty and her husband was about six years older than her so it wasn't a huge age gap. The other was seventeen and her husband was 28 when they got married. I remember bringing my maternal grandmother to visit her husband in hospital when they had been married for over 55 years. He had missed one of their daughters' wedding anniversary parties. As my grandmother expressed regret and said it was the first time she had gone to a party on her own without him, his hand sought hers and squeezed it. It was clear they still loved each other dearly. Yes, some married for love or they fell deeper in love after marriage.

Advantages of marriage for women

Many women were happy to get married even if they had never met their future husband before the match was agreed. Many secondary school children lost sympathy for Peig Sayers, having been forced to struggle through her life story "as Gaeilge". Yet many who read it in English years later find it to be an entertaining and inspiring story. When Peig Sayers considered her options of going back into service or getting married and having children, she didn't take much time to decide on the latter. She wanted her own hearth and home and she wanted to be able to sit down if she was tired rather than be at the beck and call of a mistress. Despite the fact that she had never met her future husband and had to move to an island, she put her complete trust in her older brother to take charge of the negotiations. She knew she could "neither choose one nor bar any."[38] Despite the low rate of marriage, on Peig's wedding day there were seven other weddings taking place. Weddings could not happen during the forty days of Lent so the busiest marrying season was Shrovetide, the week before Lent.

Some women had to care for parents and had to wait until they were free to marry, free from familial responsibilities and ties. Once they were free, marriage seemed like the best option:

> ### *Irish Farmers Journal* 22nd July 1972
> **Home Lover**: A refined lady in her late forties, very sincere, only recently relieved from caring for her family, would like to hear from kind, refined gentlemen. She is engaged in farming, very good family background. Many interests, RC. Confidence given and expected.

Marriage was seen to provide companionship, higher social status and the opportunity to be a mistress in your own home.

The importance of not having a potential mother-in-law is reflected below. A relatively young farmer is independent from family ties and sees himself as a good catch as a result:

> **The Irish Press, 16th October 1946**
> **Farmer, age 30, 40 acres**, own farm, no encumbrance, would like to correspond with farmer's daughter, age 25-30, good strong girl with view to above.[39]

Note that she still had to be a "good strong girl" which could be translated into "able to do all the farm work in addition to the housework and rear plenty of children". As stated in *Diary of a Matchmaker*, "a lone man in his own house is a powerful attraction", whereas if his mother or sisters shared the dwelling, it would be held against him.[40] I wonder how many women saw this young farmer as a good catch and contacted him.

If a woman married a man her own age and if his family was not provided for (if he still had to fund younger siblings or look after his parents), she was regarded as a fool as she would have to work harder than if she married an older man.[41] It seems that marrying an older man was seen as a good move by many – after all, it probably meant more money, no mother-in-law, mistress of house and he might even die soon!

Spinsterhood

On the one hand, unmarried women were not viewed as an anomoly. Yet because marriage bestowed social status, spinsters were often treated as objects of pity or scorn. Unmarried women living with unmarried siblings in parentless families were respected. However, if they were caring for parents and waiting for them to die so they could be independent, it was considered that they had lost their opportunity to emigrate or get married. While a man could still be viewed as relatively eligible in his sixties, very few women were.

Therefore, single status was not something to be proud of. In *The Ballroom of Romance*, the main character Bridie is glad to finish with the weekly routine of going to the same ballroom and seeing the same people, all in the hope of marrying one of the band singers. This meant she could give herself the status of marriage and security rather than dying as an old maid. "If you couldn't have love, the next best thing was surely a decent man."[42]

She knows she will never love Dano Ryan as much as she loved her first love but she looks forward to his company and to his help on the farm. When it becomes clear Dano will marry his landlady, she puts that dream aside. She agrees to marry Bowser Egan when his mother dies. She knows she is marrying to prevent future loneliness and to give herself some status.

It seems marriage to farmers was seen as preferable to spinsterhood for many women in mid 20th century Ireland if they could secure it.

The government are worried

The large number of unmarried farmers caused concern in the mid 20th century. At government level, Eamonn De Valera[43] realised his romantic vision of small family farms, frugal living and self–sufficiency in rural Ireland was not working out the way he had intended, and he believed farmers were going to die out. For two decades, he tried to persuade the government to fund the "dower house" scheme, where farmers would receive a grant to build a second house on the farm. He believed (as did many of its proponents) that it would encourage earlier marriage, as the elderly couple could move out of the farmhouse and leave it to the young married couple. It was argued that farmers' sons, who were living with parents, were immature, were never going to be progressive farmers and were no longer viewed as eligible by the time they inherited. De Valera wanted to see farms as family farms, with wives and children contributing to the economic unit and to its success. He wanted adult sons to have responsibility.[44]

De Valera's dower house scheme was never implemented partly due to the cost. Would it have increased the rate of marriage if it had gone ahead? Young women with a secondary school education (daughters of strong farmers) apparently weren't keen on marriage to a farmer even if his family had servants. Some wanted to be able to work after marriage and many wanted financial independence.

Others argued that it wasn't the absence of the dower house or financial restrictions that prevented farmers from marrying. Some claimed that farmers believed in the myth of 'gay bachelor' life, that they saw marriage as limiting their fun and only married when they wanted an heir for the farm.[45] Farmers were accused of being lazy and weak, and it was felt that they should be able to make their parents give up control and assume running of the farm. It was believed that rural development and farm progression were being hindered as a result.[46] For the sake of the country, farmers should be marrying and rearing families.

It was also argued that delayed marriage meant bachelors became too lazy and mean to marry. One "solution" suggested that land should be taken from these lazy bachelors (and the threat might induce them to action) to fund the marriage of young farmers. Each farmer who married should receive a marriage grant providing them with five acres of their own, a house, a couple of pigs, some poultry and £300. This money could be partly remitted on the birth of each child, which would ensure the future of Irish farming.[47] No pressure on people to have large families then!

Men for, Women against

A public debate on the topic of marriage was held in 1955[48] entitled "Do Farmers Make Good Husbands". It sounds like it would have been a good laugh – especially if one of the ladies ended up throwing something at the men as I am sure they were tempted to do. The men argued that the average farmer provided what most women expected from marriage – love, respect, the benefit of bringing up a family in a rural environment, modern amenities and a car to get to town. They saw farming wives as the most content of all wives.

The arguments against were laid by the women, stating that women had to work from dawn to dusk and were left caring for children and darning socks when he went to the pub. They argued that farmers went to the market knowing their wives would do the farm work as well as the housework and that they never remembered birthdays or anniversaries or brought home a bunch of flowers.

One female speaker advocated that marrying an old farmer was not to be recommended. Her advice was to marry them young and train them in, especially as too many were keen to install milking machines but not washing machines.

The evening closed with a comment from the chairman reflecting on how well the ladies had presented their side of the debate, especially as they themselves weren't convinced by their arguments! The Irish Countrywomen Association ladies then provided tea at the end of the evening. I wonder if they saw the irony.

Rural Marriages 1950 - 2013

Various agencies were set up to try and increase the number of marriages amongst the farming communities. Dublin's Matrimonial Bureau ran numerous advertisements in the *Irish Farmers Journal* in 1959, promising to arrange postal or personal introductions for those who genuinely sought marriage. Representations from both religions, Catholic and Protestant, were invited. They also tried to encourage ladies with farms to get in contact. The Knock Marriage Bureau was set up in 1960 to unite spinsters with eligible bachelors. By 1971, it boasted 35 marriages (mostly farmers) from 2,866 introductions, plus nine engagements and three potential engagements.[49] By 2011, it had achieved 890 marriages and one third of them included farmers. Eight men married women with their own farms.

The concern about late marriage and the number of bachelors lasted well into the 1970s and 1980s. A report in *The Irish Press* in 1971 stated that 30% of those who owned a farm were unmarried and would not have an heir. Between the shortage of potential wives (50,000 farmers' sons and less than 5,000 farmers' daughters) and the lethargy of farmers towards marriage, there was huge concern about the future of rural Ireland. Farmers seemed to wait until the land needed a woman more than they did, and they waited so long that they were no longer seen as eligible.[50]

However, as time went on, women with property felt they were in a position to choose and were more assertive in their advertising:

Irish Farmers Journal 21st December 1985
Adventurous Munster is a much travelled single lady in her thirties from farming background, working in clerical position. She would like to hear from a refined gentleman, professional or dry stock farmer from anywhere in Ireland. Must be C of I.

Maybe this woman came from a dairy farm and knew the work involved and hence stipulated a dry stock farmer. She wasn't planning to milk any cows!

While a farm was considered advantageous, it was not necessarily the deciding factor any more:

The Kerryman, 9th June 1989
Tall, dark and handsome single male, 29, farm manager, quiet, would like to meet lady with or without her own farm, with a view to marriage.

DetailedO

OK

Some farmers still appreciated a bride with a dowry though, even as recently as 1970:

> ***The Anglo Celt*** 25th **February 1970**
> **Matrimony – Cavan Farmer** with large farm and capital, desires to hear from a country girl from 26 to 32 with a view to early marriage. Some dowry.

Arranged marriages were phasing out, the dowry was replaced by a gift (cash or livestock) and weddings were forged for love. Farmers were building their own houses rather than living with parents. The marriage bar was lifted in 1973 and more farmers' wives worked outside the home. Does that mean that the image of the farmer as a "good or bad catch" changed? Of course it did.

Would You Marry A Farmer Nowadays?

Are farmers a good catch? Do they make good marriage partners? Does the prospect of "road frontage" mean the fields are paved with gold? Is living in the countryside a rural idyll? Would you marry a farmer?

Believe it or not, farmers are now "in vogue" as marriageable material, maybe more so since the Celtic Tiger died a long and tragic death between 2007-2009. While farmers close to towns and cities were raking in money selling land to developers, the majority were seen as the poor relations to builders, carpenters and plumbers during the building boom. Working long hours, being asset rich but cash poor and living in isolation just didn't quite cut the mustard in comparison to a second property in Spain and a

large new house with electric gates and a well manicured lawn.

Farming might now be described as the occupation that could save the country from ruin as agricultural exports increase. Everyone knows exports are Ireland's only means to economic recovery. That is not to say that farmers as the main producers are going to be wealthy, but their hard work and attention to detail when producing good food just might gain the recognition it deserves. Farming is now seen as a respectable occupation once again, not necessarily the pot of gold at the end of the rainbow but an occupation that provides a healthy and fulfilling lifestyle in which to rear a family.

Why you might like to marry a farmer:

1.   Most farmers have an affinity with nature – think of all those lovely walks you will enjoy as you both bring in the cows. He can give you a nature lesson on all the flora and fauna.

2.   He is not going to be away on long conference trips or spend four hours a day commuting. In fact, he is never going to be far away – he will be out in the yard, spreading fertilizer in a nearby field, milking in the parlour, fencing in a distant field. So whether you want him for something or just want some company, all you have to do is head towards the farmyard in your wellies and you are likely to find him nearby.

3.   If you have always hankered after learning how to drive a jeep or a big tractor, dating a farmer is a great opportunity to drive some big machinery. It is a good idea to learn before you actually get married as patience tends to wane rapidly once the wedding is over. He will be much more forgiving of your crashing of gears and crooked driving while in the first flush of love.

4.   Road frontage used to be the pathway to gold if farmers could sell sites for houses. Those days may be gone, but with plenty of acres, you can enjoy feeling that you are the mistress of all you survey, as you gaze towards the horizon. Just remember that some of it may still have to be paid for!

5.   He may not have time to go to the gym in town or have a black belt in karate but between pulling calves, walking after cattle, milking cows and dipping sheep, he is going to be fit and healthy. If he spends most of the day on a tractor or a quad though, go easy on those big desserts.

6.   As a farmer, he will care about his livestock and manage animals well. An affinity with animals indicates that he will be relatively patient with humans too.

7.   Farmers tend to be more the strong, silent types rather than the "talk for Ireland" variety, although there are always exceptions to the rule. They are usually good listeners (or at least, most will nod at opportune moments).

8.   A tan, even on pale Irish freckled skin, is always possible with farmers and makes them look healthy and good-looking. Do be aware though that the gorgeous tanned skin will end at the neckline and the top of the arms – otherwise known as the "farmer's tan".

9.   No false flattery. Farmers tend to be down to earth creatures and rarely flatter if they do not mean it. Therefore, when he says you look good in a new dress or new jeans, you know he means every word.

10.   Farmers are very aware of their environment, partly because they have to adhere to various practices laid down by the government departments, partly because it is second nature to them and partly because they genuinely care. Being eco-aware is trendy now. You can even manipulate the conversation with friends to swing around to farming topics by talking about environmental issues first.

11.   Is farming a rural idyll? Of course it is. Where else can you live where the only traffic noises you hear are the rattle of the silage trailers and the trundle of the milk lorry. Just bear in mind that the tweeting of birds may be overpowered by the cawing of crows.

12.   The old-fashioned and reliable family values of trust, comradeship, peace and support tend to hold tight in farming families.

13.   Vitamin D is one of those essential vitamins and some of us just do not get enough of it, particularly if we are

in offices from nine to five and commuting. Being out on the farm gains you plenty of fresh air and Vitamin D.

14.   You will enjoy panoramic views of the countryside. If you love photography, painting, horse-riding or cross country running, you could not live in a better place.

15.   While a farmer may work all hours under the sun, he is self employed and hence his own boss so he can take time off whenever he wants. This is subject only to the weather impacting crops, the calving / lambing season, the breeding season, the long milking season and the fattening season. Yes, you will get him away for about three nights in the year.

16.   You will become part of a tight-knit community. They will be fiercely loyal and will rally around if anything happens where you need help. Just remember your every move will be a topic of conversation too.

17.   Fed up of apartment living? His rambling farmhouse may not have all the latest modern conveniences but the beauty of living in a detached house where you have nobody living above, below or on either side of you is not to be sneezed at.

18.   You are likely to have a large garden. If you love gardening, you will have plenty of scope to put your stamp on it. If he likes gardening, you will always get a bunch of flowers on special occasions without him having to drive to town for them.

19.   Do you remember the 1970s sitcom *The Good Life,* with Tom & Barbara, Margo & Gerry?[51] Do you want to be the fun loving Barbara who worked hard, had little money, loved her one "good" frock and yet had a good laugh, or Margo whose life revolved around her wardrobe and her society friends? Perhaps a happy medium of hard work with the occasional night out is the best choice for most farming women – wellies by day, heels by night.

20.   If you enjoy your own company, would like to start your own business on the farm or work out in the fresh air with machinery or animals, a farmer just might be the perfect marriage partner for you.

Would you Marry a Farmer?

Why farmers may not be such a good catch:

1.	You don't just get half the value of the assets when you marry a farmer; you also get your fair share of the existing and future farm debt.

2.	Farms need constant upkeep and that means constant investment, in the good years and the bad.

3.	Those who previously lived in towns may take time to acclimatise to the fact it can be five miles to the nearest shop for a loaf of bread and some butter. Dropping into a neighbour for a cup of sugar is not something that just happens late at night in apartment blocks.

4.	Your marriage vows of "for better, for worse" also apply to the in-laws who might be living right beside you.

5.	The Irish Mammy can be a tough woman to live up to – are you prepared to try to equal her cooking and cleaning skills?

6.	For city girls, it can take time to get used to the peace (no traffic), the darkness (no street lights), the isolation (no immediate neighbours) and the muck and the dirt (no sweepers).

7.	Farmers may be asset rich but most are cash poor. Cashflow can be a struggle with fluctuating incomes – are you quite relaxed regarding your financial situation?

8.   With farming, the show always has to go on. The cows have to calve and be milked, the sheep have to be shorn, the wheat has to be harvested –even birthdays, illness or bereavement won't get in the way. Animals still have to be fed when the weather is horrible outside and you would prefer to be under the duvet.

9.   If you only like the countryside for pretty picnics fully equipped with Cath Kidston – the silage men won't appreciate pretty polka dots at all.

10.   If your idea of heaven is Grafton Street on a Saturday morning or a Thursday evening.

11.   If your idea of a mud mask is a facial treatment at a spa.

12.   If you think wellies should be pretty in pink and only be soiled by splashes of water.

13.   If city breaks for weekends away are an essential part of life – it is unlikely to happen when married to a farmer.

14.   If you think the benefits of no commute to work means your husband will be around until 8:59am and home at 5:01pm.

15.   Should you have bad asthma – straw, hay, cut grass and dusty meal are not going to be good for it.

16.   If you would feel your new kitchen should come before a new fertiliser spreader or a new milking parlour. Unfortunately, the purchase that improves the financial situation comes first.

17.   If you do not like cooking and fancy the idea of a husband who cooks all the meals (this was my main objection to returning to farming life).

18.   If you want to keep your hands soft and nails manicured.

19.   If your idea of Saturday morning bliss is a lie on, followed by a visit to the hairdressers and the beautician.

20.   If you are a private person and prefer anonymity, your life is never your own in a small community.

Do you still want to marry a farmer? Of course you do – remember what those ladies said during their debate in 1955? You can train him in!! Read on to see where you might find the perfect farmer and discover how you might hook him.

Section 2

How To Find A Good Farmer

Irish Farmers Journal 22/07/1972

Nicola Silver is an enterprising intelligent well-to-do farmer's daughter. She is 26 years, of smart, attractive appearance, cheerful and very sincere. She would like to meet a nice sincere gentleman of neat appearance, extensive farmer, business man or professional between 26-38. She has large capital and stock. Her interests are varied. Photo appreciated with first letter. Confidence assured.

The Irish Press 24/05/1971

Brown Eyes is a farmer's daughter from Co. Cork who has a good education and is considered attractive and would like to hear from respectable farmers (Protestant) aged 35-45 years. They must be good looking and of a good family. They must also be sober and capable. She likes farming and has wide interests and some capital.

Which Type of Farmer is Best?

Even though land with road frontage has significantly reduced in value,[52] farmers are now considered a good catch by many. However, there are huge differences in the types of farmers and before you go looking for one, you may want to consider which type of farmer would suit you and your lifestyle best.

Tillage farmers – Irish tillage farms are not that large; most are 100-300 acres. Tillage farmers are really busy in the spring and the autumn when sowing and harvesting. Some tillage farmers have a part-time job or another farming enterprise. Therefore, he either brings in additional off-farm income and is out of your hair, or you have lots of quality time with him during the quieter months. They like their big machines just as much as you might like handbags and expensive shoes: John D versus Jimmy C.

Sheep farmers – There is quite a lot of work with sheep between lambing, shearing, dipping, dagging, feeding and herding. Sheep farmers are particularly busy during lambing and if you marry one, you will be too. If you want an Aga or a Rayburn, expect to be sitting by it at 2am bringing tiny lambs back to life. Some farmers schedule the birth of lambs to coincide with having lambs ready for the Easter market. Hence, your calendar has to work around that timetable. Being vegetarian is never a good thing if you are a sheep farmer's wife as Easter lamb has to be one of the most delicious meats you will miss out on.

Beef farmers – Some beef farmers have suckler cows and rear the calves for sale. Others buy in cattle and finish them for the factory. While not as labour intensive as dairy farming, they are busy at certain times of the year, between winter feeding, calving and going to and from the mart or factory.

Dairy farmer – Dairy farmers probably work the longest hours, as cows have to be milked twice a day, fourteen times a week, so taking off on a spontaneous day away can be tricky. The calving period is the busiest season. When you are feeding calves or bringing in the cows together, it should all be considered good quality time spent together.

Pig farmers – Between sows farrowing, piglets being weaned and getting pigs to market, pig farming is also busy. It is an industry with tight margins so most pig farmers seem to be incredibly efficient. The only disadvantage is that pig slurry is one of the smelliest and moving grown pigs can be easier said than done.

Goat farmers – Goat farming is in vogue now as more people are drinking goats' milk and eating goats' cheese. More people are eating goat meat too so that market is growing. Goats have incredibly cheeky personalities so the farmer is bound to be patient. Otherwise, the goats will drive him to distraction and he will blow a gasket. You have to be equally tolerant and vigilant, as goats possess an incredible ability to sneak into the garden to eat roses and pull clothes off the line.

Smallholders – Many smallholders may have left the corporate rat race in the city and bought a few acres in the countryside planning to live the good life. If you are a Barbara Good, you will love the challenge of growing and producing your own food – rearing chickens, pigs and goats, and growing vegetables in a polytunnel and large garden. If you are a Margo Leadbetter though, it just might end in tears. You just have to decide if you are a Barbara or a Margo[53].

Where Do You Find Your Farmer?

The Ploughing Championships

The Ploughing Championships is one of the most important events in the Irish farming calendar – three whole days of ploughing, muck, mud, livestock, shopping, fashion and food. It started many decades ago as a ploughing competition, with diehard farmers, tractors, horses and ploughs. It is now a huge event with 80,000 people visiting each day. As you can imagine, a huge proportion are going to be farmers or wannabe rural dwellers. Do not presume you will have your pick of the farmers though. There will be lots of other women there too. You need to work out how you are going to stand out from the crowd and where exactly you should head to find the farmer of your dreams.

Big Boys and their Toys - The machinery mad men hover around the new tractors, trailers, combines and loaders. You know what they say about men with big cars; just multiply that for big tractors! If he buys a new Massey Ferguson, you won't just be sharing the ownership of it, you will be sharing the debt too.

Vintage Machinery Enthusiasts - These are proud men polishing their prize-winning 1970 Fords or 1947 Massey Fergusons. They love nostalgia and are bound to have lots of scrap metal projects dotted around the farm and house. They spend any spare time on the latest project in a draughty shed. Going on vintage tractor runs or to vintage shows on Sundays is seen as the perfect weekend activity.

Ploughing Mad - Believe it or not, lots of people go to the Ploughing Championships and do not see a plough. The ploughing section is a dedicated area away from all the shopping and stands. The participants are talented men and women who take great pride in straight lines and exact measurements. It is probable he is a "belts and braces" kind of guy, and is unlikely to leave anything to chance. If you are more of a "slap dash, it'll do" kind of gal, don't go near the ploughing area looking for a farmer. To be honest, he will probably be concentrating so much on the competition that you will have to think up a very inventive strategy to get him to notice you. Learning to plough could be a tactic!

A Farmer Foodie - Food Demonstration Tents tend to be incredibly busy. It is amazing how many people want to learn how to make boxty or cook a leg of lamb. These tents are usually filled to capacity with women. If there is a man in there, he is a brave one and is bound to be a good cook. You will have stiff competition to nab him.

Animal Section - Livestock farmers are passionate about their favourite breed of cattle, sheep or pigs. Not only is he a good handler, he knows how to shampoo, blowdry and coiffeur a pedigree bull to within an inch of its life. He may have been a Nicky Clarke or an Andrew Collinge in a previous existence. Will you let him style your hair though? That is the question.

IFA Tent - He may be a budding politician hidden in farmer's clothing as he catches up on the political and farming gossip in the IFA tent. It tends to be particularly busy if it is an election year. Remember that farmers cum politicians are never at home – there is always a meeting to attend.

How to attract the right attention at the Ploughing!

You can adopt various methods to stand out from the crowd and get noticed. If it is wet, there are plenty of puddles, mud and muck. Teenagers seem to enjoy throwing each other into the wet mud and having a good roll, finishing in a mudfight. I'm not so sure that the mud from the ploughing match is the best application for the skin, but they get lots of attention as they walk around splattered from head to toe. The Ploughing Championships doesn't have a "Ladies Day" or "Best Dressed Lady" (too much mud), but dressing appropriately for the weather is essential. Wearing high heels will invite ridicule, so the right choice of wellies is crucial for your success.

What your wellies say about you

Brand new wellies with polka dots or zebra stripes might make any busy farmer run a mile unless of course, he is after a trophy wife. They suggest you bought them especially for the event and have never possessed a pair of wellies before. Either borrow a pair of well worn ones or wear them constantly on woodland walks for a month beforehand so they look broken in.

Bright or floral wellies that are well worn and carry the mud stains of the Electric Picnic or woodland walks will receive some approval. You may not be of farming stock but you are fashionable and not afraid of getting dirty. You will be

Would you Marry a Farmer?

viewed as perfect for the farmer who wants a hardworking wife and you are also demonstrating that you scrub up well.

Plain grey/blue/green Dunbar wellies purchased at the local creamery will convey that you are a farmer's daughter, often out working on the farm and well able for a busy farming life. Being practical and hard-wearing boots and yet relatively inexpensive, they will signify your matter-of-fact, down-to-earth personality perfectly.

Hunter wellies suggest that you love horses and you will cost him a fortune in equine-related expenses. In order to avoid future financial strife, look for a farmer who is also wearing this brand of Wellington boot. Of course, they may also signify that you have fallen arches and need good arch support!

The Mart

Farmers descend on marts every week in their droves, buying, selling, sussing out the prices or having a chat, you could be spoilt for choice. What proportion are single and what proportion won't have their Mammy with them I cannot say, but it is certainly a place to sit and view the talent. Very few women go to the marts in Ireland, so you will definitely be in the minority. On a positive note, you will have the pick of the bunch.

The older farmers sit on the tiered seating around the far edge of the ring. While many of them are buying or selling, they also use the opportunity to catch up on the latest news with their comrades. These farmers spend half the week going to various markets – partly for a social life, partly because it is their bread and butter and partly because it is almost an addiction to see what price animals are making. A circle of farmers stands right beside the ring, leaning against it with their shoulders hunched so they can see under the highest bar. Another line of farmers leans against the back wall looking rather nonchalant, yet keep a very close eye on proceedings.

Older farmers look weather-beaten and lined, yet appear content to be there on their "day out". Those in their seventies and eighties wear brown or black suit jackets and their walking sticks double as cattle sticks. Most wear checked caps or trilby hats. Old scuffed shoes or wellies finish off the ensemble.

Those in their fifties and sixties are more casually dressed, most wearing a respectably clean and ironed shirt and jumper. Many have a "married" look, judging by their tidy appearance. Blues and browns seem to be the "uniform" colours for this age group. The occasional one wears full length blue overalls. They chat quietly and watch the proceedings with interest.

The younger farmers are very mixed in appearance. Some appear scruffy and are unshaven, with sloppy jumpers or untidy polo shirts, their hair needing a trim. It is hard to decide whether they are either too lazy or too busy to keep themselves tidier. Having a look at the calluses on their hands will reveal the truth. Some may wear denim jeans that are clean, but reveal the faded marks of farmyard muck that just didn't quite wash out.

Others are well turned out and may be part-time farmers, as their clothing seems more contemporary and trendy. Maybe they are influenced by working with others and seeing different fashion trends. An occasional farmer sports a red jacket, the only bright colour in the large area. Polo shirts and T-shirts dominate.

Are there any gentry farmers? There is the occasional farmer in a smart checked shirt with corduroy trousers. One or two farmers wear smart jeans with a faux Barbour type jacket and you may find yourself giving them a second glance, wondering if they are impersonators or if they really are farmers.

There is tension in the air despite the noise of banter and lively chat. The buyers know their profits for the year will be squeezed if they buy at too high a price or if they buy animals that will not thrive as effectively as others. The sellers know what it costs to produce the animal, but realise that the price is driven by the market as well as by the quality of their animals. If they are selling a substantial number, €50 either way on each animal can make a significant difference to their profit.

If you go to the mart, you will be one of a minority of women there, hence you may receive plenty of attention. Your choice of attire and wellies becomes even more paramount as a result. Some women have met their husbands at the mart, believe it or not – the men went looking for a heifer or some bull calves and found a wife. Quite a good day's work really, all things considered.

If you are planning to leave before the mart is over, remember to park near the gateway when you arrive. Otherwise, you may find that your car has been barricaded in typical Irish fashion. Farmers presume that everyone stays until it is over, never thinking that someone might want to leave during the sale.

Horse Races & Show Jumping

Placing bets, chatting with neighbours and other farmers, having a drink in the bar, enjoying the atmosphere – most farmers like nothing better than a good day out at the races, whether they own a horse or not. The point to point events play host to lots of local guys who are salt-of-the-earth types. Go along and give your posh wellies another outing. An occasion like the Galway Races or the Dublin Horse Show is perfect and you can really try to impress by going on Ladies Day and winning the prize for most suitably dressed lady. What man would say no to a woman who can dress impeccably and strut her stuff in wellies as well as heels?

Matchmaking Festivals

For a small country, Ireland has its fair share of matchmaking festivals. The main one is in Lisdoonvarna every September. Once the harvest is in, bachelor farmers head there in their droves to meet ladies who are looking for an Irish farmer. People come from all over the world hoping to meet the love of their lives. There is stiff competition from other ladies, but if you contact Willie Daly, the fourth generation matchmaker with his 150 year old ledger of matches and prospects, your chances of success will surely increase.

Many couples have met and married as a result of the Lisdoonvarna Matchmaking Festival. As Willie says, the festival has a good success rate because people are attuned to the signs of attraction in the air. Sometimes it is the right atmosphere and mood that makes all the difference when people are receptive to the idea of love. The fact that people are looking for love is out in the open. This means the possibilities for romance are endless. Go primed with a good chat up line, plenty of energy for late night dancing and some cash in your pocket for the craic in the pubs.

Personal Columns

Advertising in personal columns in local or national newspapers for a suitable partner has been popular for decades. Men were much more likely to advertise in the early and mid twentieth century, but now women seem to be advertising more – it just shows that so many consider a farmer to be a good catch! You do need to read between the lines to determine their true character.

> *Freemans Journal* 27th **March 1917**
> **Matrimony** Farmer bachelor RC with ready cash, over £1,500, desires introduction to young lady, with farm in her own right, best references, clerical and lay.

This man saw himself as a gift to any woman. While he considered himself well off, she had to have her own means and he was not going to share his bounty with her. What was hers would become his on marriage. This was not a case of meeting for afternoon tea in a hotel, it was an interview, with references expected and provided. Perhaps parish priests were in the habit of providing character references to those entertaining the prospect of marriage in the early twentieth century.

Anglo Celt 25th **February 1950**
Matrimony – A farmer with large farm and capital, desires to hear from a country girl from 26 to 32 with view to early marriage. Some dowry, Box 1519 Cavan.

This farmer was looking for a bride with her own dowry. It did not have to be substantial, but he was stating that his own farm was sizeable. He wasn't going to marry for love alone and acted as though he could pick and choose based on the value of the dowry. The fact that there was a bountiful supply of bachelor farmers looking for wives in the 1950s did not seem to have affected his belief that he would find a suitably dowried wife. There is no mention of his age, but the fact he wanted early marriage suggests he recently decided that he, and the land, required a woman. I suspect his mother had just died and he needed someone to wash his smelly socks and feed the calves.

Irish Farmers Journal 6th **August 1977**
Co. Waterford Lover is a tall dark and handsome farmer. Working on his mother's farm, would like to meet girl with own farm and car or a teacher. He likes country music and dancing. All replies welcome.

It sounds like this man was under his mother's thumb and was trying to wriggle out by finding a wife with her own farm or her own means. After all, if she was a teacher, that generated the same income as twenty cows in the 1970s and he wouldn't have to milk them.

The Kerryman 9th June 1989
Tall, dark and handsome single male, 29, farm manager, quiet, would like to meet lady with or without her own farm, with a view to marriage.

Working as a farm manager, this man wished to own a farm and viewed a wife with her own property as a means to get one. He seemed to realise they were few and far between, or he had become less fussy than his predecessors.

As time went on, farmers seemed to become less arrogant in their attitudes and their advertising. They described themselves in a more attractive light, perhaps realising they needed to sell themselves more if they wanted a response.

Irish Farmers Journal 13th July 2013
Shy, kind, single male, mid 50s, likes most things, seeks much younger, local, sexy Pilipino (sic) female for friendship, love and intimate relationship. N Cork.

Hmmm, I'm not sure how many Filipino ladies read the *Irish Farmers Journal.* I can't imagine anyone else replying to this one.

Irish Farmers Journal 13th July 2013
Male 60, WLTM discreet lady for fun times.

This guy sounds like he is married. It is short on words too – he is not going to be a big spender.

Irish Farmers Journal 13th **July 2013**
Male late 40s slim-medium build, own home/farm, likes walks, reading, nights in/out, seeks female 30-42 with similar interests. Midlands.

He sounds like a nice genuine bachelor farmer who might have recently inherited his farm. He is probably spending a lot of money modernising it and will have just purchased a new tractor and quad.

Irish Farmers Journal 17th **September 2013**
Single male, farmer, genuine, honest, seeks attractive female for friendship, maybe more.

As he provides very little information, this is either his first advertisement or he's trying to be secretive. There are no clues about his age, location or type of farmer. Very shy.

Somewhat ironically, given that you might expect people to be more forward in the 21st century, advertisements are much less forward now in terms of seeking a strong relationship. They ask for "friendship, maybe more" rather than marriage. Apart from marriage being a prerequisite for sexual relations in most cases a century ago, farmers wanted the security of a wife and an heir so marriage had to be on the cards.

Gay Relationships

Gay relationships are still referred to as "friends seeking friends", even in 2013. The advertisements were much more guarded half a century ago.

Irish Independent 12th December 1967
Farmer Wanted, wanted by a respectable bachelor, farm 20-50 acres, residential holding to buy or rent, could be arranged for seller to live on with purchaser if so desired.

This seems a very circumspect way to look for a gay partner. In *Confessions of a Matchmaker*, JB Keane includes a character in his sixties who asks the matchmaker for a wife and in the next breath asks for a young man. The matchmaker tells him to make up his mind before he can do anything for him.[54] It highlights the secretive way in which homosexuality was (and still is) hidden from public view in rural Ireland.

Irish Country Living 7th September 2013
50 yr old part time farmer, seeks genuine, outgoing country man 35-65, happy in wellington boots.

People can be hesitant to "come out" in rural areas, nervous about how family and friends will react to the news. While coming out is a decision that is up to the individual, those who have married or live with their partner of the same sex report that once the initial flurry of gossip has settled, most people seem to accept it.[55] The call for a referendum on same sex marriage may be the key to seeing general acceptance throughout Ireland. Men looking for men now advertise in the *Irish Country Living* supplement of *Irish Farmers Journal* but it is rare to see women advertising for a female partner.

Country Tea Dances

Country tea dances are still held around the countryside and are advertised in publications such as *Irish Country Living*. They have modernised somewhat from the lonely halls by the roadside with their pink facades and pink swing-doors of Trevor's *The Ballroom of Romance*, but the dance rooms still possess a certain country charm.

> "The dance-hall, where shadows were cast on pale-blue walls and light from a crystal bowl was dim, was shabby and tatty when the lights were switched on".[56]

Trevor describes some young girls just out of school and excited at the prospect of meeting youths at the dance on a Saturday night. Most girls attending the weekly dance and hoping for marriage know that their dancing partners will never marry, at least not until their mammies are dead. Even the motherless bachelors are set in their ways and it will take a lot to rouse them to marry. The younger men are planning to emigrate. The females know they themselves have an expiry date for marriage and a family. Wanting the status of marriage, they become more desperate with each passing week. The oldest girl there is ridiculed because she is 39, with younger girls sniggering that she should accept her single condition and not make herself a figure of fun going after men who just wanted to stay single.

Bridie, aged 36, is the heroine of the short story. She knows it won't be long until she becomes a figure of fun at the dance too. On agreeing to marry Bowser Egan, she has the comfort of knowing she will never be humiliated at the dance-hall again. Bridie knows the marriage will not happen until Bowser's mother is dead and he has sold the farm and drank the proceeds. She will marry him then as the alternative is to live alone after her father dies. It is too late to emigrate or to find another to marry. Trevor paints a bleak picture of rural Ireland for those who aspire to marriage.

I met my farmer for the first time in 1987, at a country disco in a rural community hall, not too dissimilar to the Ballroom of Romance. The only way these halls had updated from the "country dances" of the 1960s was with the presence of a DJ rather than a band. The hall was dimly lit with flashing lights from the stage, the glitter ball from the ceiling, and random flashes of bright light from the toilet doors as they opened and shut. There was no bar of any kind, not even a scheduled break for "minerals and club milks"! Those not dancing remained seated or standing by the walls in small groups. I still remember two friends sitting down with their arms folded, looking rather indignant. Two farmers had asked them to dance and on being refused, had retorted that the girls should bring their knitting the next time!

When I saw my future husband, I was sitting down chatting to others; it was still considered early at around 11pm and people were coming in. The music was blaring and there were a few girls dancing. Sharing lifts, four or five people would come in together, girls going to meet other friends, guys nodding to each other by the wall and talking about farming. Most were in their late teens or twenties. Men in their 30s or early 40s were regulars, the shy ones standing by the wall rarely asking anyone to dance, and the eternal optimists asking one girl after another, never giving up hope that a girl would stay with them.

The minute I saw my future farmer, I knew there was something about him. He was reasonably trendy for a farmer yet I knew he wasn't a townie. He had a twinkle in his eye and a cute dimple; he was relatively tall and just caught my attention.

"Do you know who that guy is?" I asked the girl beside me, trying to sound as casual as I could.

"Oh, he's my cousin" she replied, and proceeded to tell me how wonderful he was.

Once she mentioned that he was a good cook, I was hooked! However, it was almost another full year before we started going out!

Young Farmer Organisations

If you are under 35, Macra na Feirme is the perfect place to meet a potential partner, at their various events and meetings all across the country[57]. With events such as public speaking, performing arts, community events and organised travel holidays, there are plenty of opportunities for good craic and meeting your future spouse. Not only have there been lots of "Macra" weddings but 33% of those questioned in a survey said they expected to meet their life partner in Macra! Once you reach 35 though, your membership ends and the alternatives seem to be the IFA or ICA.

The farming organisations in Northern Ireland are similar. The Young Farmers Club of Ulster is for those aged 12-30. You do not have to be a farmer to join, just have an interest in rural living. Activities range from dancing to silage making, public speaking to tractor driving and football to stock judging. The organisations for those over 30 tend to be divided on gender too – with there being women in the

Women's Institute and mostly men in the Ulster Farmers Union.

The opportunity for meeting the opposite sex at farming-associated meetings diminishes significantly once you are over 35. Rural Ireland needs Macra and YFCU-plus organisations.

WWOOF

WWOOF stands for "world wide opportunities on organic farms". Volunteering to work on organic farms around the world is one way to see different farming practices as well as getting your bed and board as you travel. It might be a way to meet a charming farmer too, especially if you don't mind where in the world you end up farming.

Online Dating Websites

You might think it is difficult to find a farmer on an online dating site, but there are many to choose from on Muddy Matches. It caters for men and women living in rural areas (in UK and Ireland).[58] Designed for those looking to meet someone leading a "muddy boots" lifestyle, it seems to be a smaller and more personal dating website than others. Most of the men and women listed on it are involved in agriculture to some extent and are looking for someone with a similar passion for the great outdoors.

The advantage of online dating is you can check him out online before you meet him, bearing in mind that the photograph just might be twenty years old. According to *The Last Matchmaker*, a correspondence between two suitors, she

28 and he of unknown age, ended in surprise when they met. She had requested a photograph and he sent the only one he had ever had taken. The fact that it was taken forty years previously never occurred to him and she left the moment she saw him. She did decide to give him a second chance, as she missed his letters and they ended up getting married, but I would imagine the shock would be too much for most women.

Some of the avatars on the dating websites can look like mug shots taken at a garda station. Perhaps everyone using a dating site should get a professional photographer to take a flattering yet accurate photograph.

Farmers' Markets

A popular farmers' market is the ideal place to meet local producers of food. After all, if a farmer sells directly to market, it is likely he will be there. You can develop a huge enthusiasm for farm fresh vegetables, organic meat or apple juice until he notices you.

Charity Fun Events

Farmers are usually game for a laugh and a bit of craic. Therefore, many charity organisations are targeting farmers to help them raise money, and they can be a great way to meet a nice farmer. You could try a leisurely sponsored walk, or if you fancy being more adventurous or are looking for a fitter farmer, go on a sponsored trekking holiday. "Farmer Wants a Wife" events, which play on the format of the popular TV programmes, are springing up around the country too – no better place to meet an eligible farmer.

Blogging

This is online dating with a difference and what's more, it works! I have heard of at least one American city girl marrying an Irish farmer because she stumbled across his blog and they fell in love.

Those who blog tend to wax lyrical about the beauties of farming: the fresh crisp mornings, the birth of calves and lambs, green fields, flower filled meadows, meandering laneways, the blackberry and honeysuckle filled hedges and the funny characteristics of some animals. The photographs of charming stone calf houses do not reveal that they have to be cleaned out with a pitchfork rather than a digger. The hay bales that look so much fun to jump on disguise the fact that it takes hours to load them and bring them to the shed. The picnic dinners in the field don't disclose that they are not romantic dining but an often rushed affair. Considering you marry the farm along with the farmer, reading his blog is a good way to get to know both of them, as long as you take it all with a pinch of salt.

Starting conversation with a blogging farmer is easy. You just write a comment on his blog and he will reply. Who knows what might happen next?

Twitter

More and more farmers are tweeting, so twitter is a great way to meet an eligible farmer. Look for them during the agricultural tweetchats such as #agchat and #agchatirl each week. Farmers are using twitter to ask other farmers questions and to exchange some banter, so it is a great way to suss out his sense of humour too. You can usually tell a great deal about him from his avatar (picture), his bio and his tweets. Follow him, send him a tweet and see where it takes you – just don't stalk him!

What To Look For In A Good Farmer Husband

Farmer Chat Up Lines

Finding a guy with a chat up line that is not corny, cheesy or too darn cheeky isn't necessarily easy. You want to hear a chat up line that will compliment you and make you smile. Some will make a woman want to run a mile. Others, if said with a twinkle in the eye, just might work.

Here is a selection of classic chat-up lines that have been uttered in the not too distant past:

"Would you like me to rattle your chassis?"

"Do you fancy a cut of my trashing (threshing) machine?"

Him "Are you a Flahavans or Odlums girl?
Her "Huh? What?"
Him "Wondering what type of porridge to make you."

"Those are some fine arms for carrying buckets up the yard."

"You've got a great herding technique."

"Have you much in the way of road frontage?"

"God must have been in a good mood the day he made you."

Would you Marry a Farmer?

"How would you like to be buried with my people?"

"You look in fine fettle – I'd say you like your spuds."

And some more modern, albeit rather corny, chat up lines:

"Are you in the mooooood for a date?"

"My friends say I am outstanding in my field."

"You have the power to mooooove me."

"I'd be very ploughed if you would go on a date with me."

"I'll only be calf a man if you don't go on a date with me."

Maybe a man who is genuine, honest and direct and simply says "You're lovely" is best!

What to look out for:

How do you know if he is going to be a good 'un or not? Here are some tell-tale signs to determine the quality of the future farmer husband potential.

1. Does he treat you like a princess – at least on the first date? Does he act the perfect gentlemen by holding open the restaurant door for you and offering you his jacket if it is cold?

2. Some farmers have a reputation for being mean. Does he cringe as he pays for the first date or does he whip out the visa card without any delay?

3. Does he arrive bestowing a bunch of flowers occasionally, even if they are just from the garden? This might be a good indicator of future anniversary gifts.

4. Even if he is late because he has been working for the last eighteen hours, does he still arrive because he really wants to see you? As long as he is showered and shaved, do forgive him. If he arrives unshaven and scruffy however, it is a bit of a no-no.

5. Does he praise your cooking or does he comment on it by saying "My mammy makes it with xxxx"? You need to knock that out of him or you will hear it for evermore.

6. Does he text when he is going to be late? Being late is almost synonymous with farming but he should text at some point (although being elbow deep in grease from a tractor or calving mucus is a good excuse).

7. If he asks you to wear your best Sunday frock when meeting his parents for the first time – is he thinking of you as marriageable material?

8. If his car or jeep smells of damp dog and has medicine bottles, stray calf nuts and baler twine scattered around the floor, he may need to invest in a separate car or an occasional valet service.

9. Asking you to drop a jar of calf faeces to the vet laboratory on your way to town might be going a little too far in the early days of a relationship. However, it may signify that he feels at home in your company, though he might be taking you for granted already.

10. Does he surprise you occasionally with a day out or finish work early for a change? If he does, he really is a romantic at heart.

11. Is he appreciative when you turn up at the field with a flask of tea and some cake?

12. Does he show enthusiasm for your interests too – even if they are a million miles from farming? If he listens to you talking about fashion, decorating, girlfriends or social media for hours on end, he is showing positive signs of being a good listener.

13. If he gives you wellies as a birthday gift, do not throw them at him – not for a few minutes anyway. After all, they could be symbolic of a key to the milking parlour. Check inside to see if a bottle of fine perfume or a piece of jewellery have been hidden deep down inside the wellington boot. If there isn't anything there, feel free to

practise your wellie throwing skills with him as the target.

Note to the farmer: If you are reading this, these tips will work for impressing your girlfriend and convincing her you are capable of being a great farming husband.

The Language of Farming

When you visit a farm, you hear words that almost sound like a different language. They are not necessarily local dialect or swear words either. Farmers use particular terms, expecting them to be known by everyone, and look askance when you query what it means. If you can use these words with proficiency, particularly when in the presence of future in-laws, everyone will be most impressed with your farming knowledge.

Farming Term	What It Is Not	What It Is
Testing Cattle	It is not a case of testing their speed, even if they have broken out of a field.	It checks if cattle have tuberculosis or brucellosis. Expect anxious faces on the morning of THE TEST.
A paddock	Not just for horses.	A fenced section of a field.
Car road	Not for cars.	A wide path through the fields for tractors and cows.
A yoke	Not the yolk of an egg.	A yoke is anything the farmer can't recall the name of.
A graip	Not a misspelling of grape.	A three or four pronged pitchfork, also known in some parts as a sprong.
Zero grazing	It does not mean the cattle are not eating grass.	The cows don't go to the fields to graze; the grass is brought to them in a 'zero grazer' machine.
Felon	Not a burglar or criminal.	Mastitis. This is an infection that occurs in the mammary glands and often needs antibiotics to cure it.
Lost a quarter	Not a quarter of a dollar.	A cow's udder is divided into four quarters. Mastitis can kill the mammary glands in a quarter causing it to go dry, thereby "losing a quarter".
Agitating	Disturbing but not in the way you might think.	Agitating slurry means stirring it so thicker slurry at the top mixes with the watery slurry underneath to get a runny consistency.
Elder	Not older or wiser than you.	A cow's udder.

Dug	Not a hole in the garden.	A cow's udder.
Stores	Not a trip to the shops.	Yearling cattle that are being sold.
CAP	Not a hat or a contraceptive.	The Common Agricultural Policy as set down by the EU.
A lock	Not necessarily a padlock.	A lock is whatever can be carried in your cupped hands or in your arms. A lock of calf nuts is very different to a lock of sticks for the fire.
Dyke	Not a lesbian.	A long, deep hole to allow water to drain away.
Wraps	Not slimming wraps for animals.	Silage wraps – when grass is cut, baled and wrapped with polythene to keep it protected.
Diet feeder	Talk about an oxymoron. It implies slimming and feeding up.	A machine that chops and mixes silage, straw, beet and meal for cattle consumption.
Hen's teeth	Not sharp canines.	Very rare.
Dose	Not a cold.	Medicine administered to animals orally or via injection.
Donkey's years	Not referring to age.	A very long time. "I haven't seen her for donkey's years".
Strip wire	Not to do with a strip club.	An electric wire dividing a field into smaller areas.
Locked up	It doesn't mean he has been in prison.	If some of the farm animals are found to have tuberculosis, animals cannot be moved to another holding.
Savage Cut	Not a cut to the hand.	Heavy cut of silage (good yield).
Creep	Not a horrible person or crawling along on your hands and knees.	Feed that is provided to young stock e.g. lambs, and their mothers are prevented from eating it.

Sexual Terms	What It Does Not Mean	What It Means
Artificial insemination	Not quite an IUI for cows.	An AI technician inserts frozen semen from a male into a female. A cow could have many calves and yet, in theory, could still be a virgin.
Bull man	Not from the film *The Field*.	The Artificial Inseminator.
Straws	Not a straw bale or even "the last straw".	The semen used in artificial insemination is stored in straws.
Is she "on"?	Not sitting on something.	Is she on heat? Is she at her fertile time?
A bulling	Not referring to being angry	Is she on heat? Is she ready for the bull?
She's "wanting away"	Not to be confused with "she's wasting away".	She is on heat so wants to go to the bull (or ram or billy goat).
Synchronise	Does not refer to swimming or dancing in unison.	When heifers or cows are treated with hormones so all are on heat and can be "AI"ed at the same time.
Cranger	Not crazy.	A colloquial terms for a burdizzo which is used for castrating older animals.
Flushing	Not referring to the toilet.	When you bring sheep into season (on heat) by giving them a poor pasture followed by lush grass.
Tupping	Not to rhyme with tipping.	Mating of sheep (tup is also a male sheep).

Gender Terms	What It Does Not Mean	What It Means
Bull	Not rubbish or a papal decree.	A male that is left entire (not castrated).
Steer	Not referring to how you drive.	A castrated male bovine (also called a bullock).
Heifer	Not necessarily an insult.	A female bovine – called a heifer until she has her second calf, then she is called a cow.
Freemartin heifer	Not a member of a strange cult.	A heifer that is twin to a bull and is likely to be infertile (due to the testosterone in the womb).
A maiden heifer	Not an old maid.	A heifer that hasn't had a calf yet.
A Mullingar heifer	Not necessarily from Mullingar.	Mullingar is reputed to have great fattening land so it means a heifer that has thrived well.
Ram	Not hitting something.	A male sheep, used for breeding purposes. A tup.
Wether	Not a misspelling of "weather".	A castrated older male lamb destined for the factory. Wether hoggets are also destined for the factory.
Ewe	Not a misspelling of "you".	Female sheep which has had lambs.
Gilt	Not to be confused with guilt.	A young female pig that has not had piglets.
Dam	Not for storing water.	An animal's mother.
Sire	Not a term of respect.	An animal's father

Pregnancy & Birth Terms	What It Does Not Mean	What It Means
Springing	Not jumping about.	A mammal is described as 'springing' when her udder fills with milk before giving birth.
A Springer	Not a springer spaniel.	A bovine that is going to calve soon.
Pins are down	It doesn't refer to sewing or bowling.	The ligaments on either side of her tail relax before she goes into labour.
Humouring	Not a stand up comedian slot.	The cow is "humouring" to calve.
Cleanings	Not what is left after washing down a cow for a show.	Refers to the afterbirth / placenta.
Blabs out	Not a child cartoon.	The fluid filled membrane (also called a water bag) which comes out at the start of labour.
Beastings	It is not a bee sting.	Calves don't have any immunity when they are born; hence, it is extremely important that they drink their mothers' first milk, otherwise known as colostrum or beastings.
Dirty cows	It is not suggesting they are rude or filthy.	Refers to a cow holding on to her "cleanings" and having a uterine infection.
Empty cows	It does not mean the cows are hungry.	It means the cow is not pregnant or perhaps she lost the calf.

Submission	Not referring to anything in *50 Shades of Grey*.	Refers to pregnancy rates. The percentages of cows that are AI'd or bulled during the breeding months.
Calving interval	Not the break the farmer gets between calving cows.	The number of days between the birth of one calf and the birth of the next.
Yaneing	Not a type of moaning.	A colloquial term for when sheep are having lambs.
Body condition score	This is not referring to anyone's svelte figure.	Cows should attain a certain condition score to maximise chances of pregnancy and to ensure a healthy pregnancy and safe birth. The score refers to her 'fat cover'.

The Perfect Farming Wife – What Is She Like?

Home Economics textbooks in the 1950s had plenty of tips for how to be the perfect wife. They were mostly intended for the wife of an office worker. They recommended that she ensure a hot meal was ready when her beloved husband came home from work, that she had re-applied her makeup and was smiling when he walked in the door, surrounded by clean, well-dressed and quiet children. She should not complain if he was late or grumpy. She had to enquire about his day, rub his feet and submit to his demands. She had to delay removing her makeup and putting in hair rollers until after he fell asleep (in case she frightened him with her appearance).

I wonder what those manuals would have prescribed for a perfect farming wife. Would she have had to put on her makeup before milking the cows, feeding the calves, collecting eggs and getting breakfast? Might she have had to run the farm efficiently while he was at the mart and greet him with a smile when he returned from an afternoon in the pub? Would she have been required to feed pigs, haul water from the well, wash clothes, feed children, help them with homework, milk cows, feed calves, and have a hot dinner for him when he returned from the fields? And in the evenings, when all the children were in bed and he was relaxing in front of the fire, would she have had to darn socks and knit jumpers while asking him about his day? Oh hang on though, with the exception of the makeup and maybe the smile, most farmers' wives did all that.

The prescribed perfect wife may have altered significantly in the six decades since those Home Economics textbooks were published, but farming families will have their own idea of the perfect farming wife.

Perfect Farm Wife as per the Farmer:

- Washes, dries, and folds his farming clothes, leaving them in a neat pile where he can find them.
- Pairs and mends his work socks.
- Has his "good clothes" left out ready for "good" occasions; this saves him having to work out what to wear.
- Makes sure that nutritious and filling meals are ready on time – whatever time that may be.
- Flexible and prepared to run errands if required.
- Keeps the house and garden tidy.
- Prepared to muck in and help when needed.
- Scrubs up well for the occasional night on the town.
- Be an eternal optimist even when the bank balance is so red, it is scarlet.
- Loving and caring to animals as well as humans.
- Able to find the piece of paper he left at the end of the table three days ago.
- Good at budgeting and managing the cashflow situation.
- Never moves his stack of farming newspapers and AI catalogues from wherever he leaves them.

Perfect Farm Wife as per the Father-in-Law:

- Able to muck in (i.e. do the work of a man).
- A natural at calf feeding and lamb delivering.
- Understands the farming lingo and uses it coherently.
- Able to drop everything to go and pick up a tractor part.

- Uses the same bank, accountant and agricultural companies that he always used.
- Able to produce an heir and a spare.

Perfect Farm Wife as per the Mother-in-Law:

- Looks after her son well: keep his clothes clean and ironed, provide good home cooked meals with plenty of home baking to sustain him.
- Able to produce an heir and a spare.
- Grateful to her for his existence.
- Capable of feeding calves and delivering lambs at the very least.
- Working outside the home is fine (especially if she did it) but you must work on the farm in the evenings and at weekends.
- Keeps the house clean and tidy; the mother-in-law (MIL) will note any significant expenses on the house or your wardrobe.
- Keeps the garden free of weeds.
- Able to feed contractors at a moment's notice.
- Has dinner at exactly the same time every day – just as she did.
- Always has a batch of fresh scones or a cake on standby should any sales reps, neighbours or friends call.
- Willing to take over her role in community events (eventually), starting with the church flower rota. She will be secretly relieved to pass these to you but you are expected to be grateful.

Do You Have Farmer's Wife Potential?

It is not all about learning the lingo, there is more to being a farmer's wife or becoming a fully fledged farmerette than meets the eye. If you can pass some of these tests after a couple of months in his company, you are well on the way.

Marrying a farmer is not just about falling in love with him and he with you. You marry the farm when you marry the farmer; therefore, it is also about embracing the farming way of life and finding your own position within it. Even if you continue working in the city and scarcely know what a cow looks like, you will see him a lot more and enjoy each other's company if you head out to the yard to stop a gap or for a tractor ride occasionally.

This list does come with one word of warning though – once he sees you can accomplish a job to his exacting standards, it is considered to be "your job" for evermore.

How many Tasks can you accomplish?

- Can you carry two four-gallon buckets of milk to calves multiple times for the morning and evening feeds?

- Are you able to assist at a Caesarean section and not wince as you see the sirloin steak cut of muscle being stitched?

- Can you hold a womb in your gloved hands while it is being stitched without fainting or grimacing?

- Can you create a meal for working men who suddenly arrive at the farm from the few items in the fridge? Ingredients might be half a sliced pan, an onion, three apples, a carrot, half a pack of rashers and a lump of cheese. If you can dash to the chicken coop for a few eggs and to the milking parlour for milk, you can create a perfect omelette or even something more creative (or boiled eggs and toast in my case). It's the farming version of "Ready, Steady, Cook".

- Are you capable of driving a tractor in a straight line?

- Do you know how to reverse a trailer through a narrow gateway without hitting the gateposts?

- Can you deliver lambs or goat kids?

- Are you happy swopping nail varnish for calluses and welts during the lambing and calving season?

- Do you know how to stop a gap?

- Can you milk a cow, goat, sheep or mare?

- Do you understand and appreciate the many uses of baler twine? Examples can include tying up dogs and goats, holding up trousers, acting as firelighters, tying gates ...

- Can you carry a bag of feed on your shoulder?

- Are you capable of stacking small bales on a trailer while on a hill?

- Can you dose and inject livestock?

- Can you run faster than cattle?

- Would you enjoy the challenge of bringing a tiny lamb back to life by keeping it warm and feeding it every few hours?

- Are you able to teach newborn calves how to drink milk from a teat or a bucket?

You now know which type of farmer might suit you best, where to find him and how to make him notice you. You realise what is involved in dating a farmer, meeting his parents and keeping them all impressed with your presence and your knowledge. You understand what might be involved in living on a farm and you are still with me. Good woman - next up are the tips for dating a farmer, what you need to know!

Would you Marry a Farmer?

Section 3

Dating a Farmer
What You Need To Know

The Irish Times 24th **April 1888**

A Farmer living in Ireland wishes to hear from a lady with a view to marriage. Advertiser has a farm and premises suitable for any of his class, and worth at least 300l. Respondent must have some money to enable both to keep a good house, must know some music and be a good singer. Age from 20 to 40 will do. Advertiser is 35. Reply to C83....

The Reality Of Dating A Farmer

Being courted by a farmer can be very different to going out with someone working in another industry, particularly if you have only dated people working in 9-5 jobs before. Farmers can be a different breed, not just because of their lifestyle choice. Farming involves working up to twenty hours a day at busy times and it is seldom much less than 365 days a year. However, it is a wonderful way of life and many farmers' wives say they can not imagine doing anything else.

You will have fun helping out on the farm, which can be beautifully romantic on a summer's day as you stroll across flower strewn meadows together, but not so joyful when you are assisting at a difficult birth at midnight in a freezing cold cowshed, rounding up livestock in lashing rain or trying to find sheep in the snow.

In farming, there is nearly always something to make you laugh even if it takes a while to see the humour in some situations. You may feel indignant if your wellies get stuck in the muck and you have the choice of leaving the wellies behind and going barefoot or waiting to be pulled out but you will laugh at yourself eventually. The same goes if you accidentally drive the quad or the tractor into a situation you can't get out of and need someone to rescue you and the vehicle.

While he may work long hours, the advantage is he is almost always around. It is a case of you taking the time to go to the farmer rather than waiting for him to be ready on time.

You have a choice – read and decide to go for it or read and run a hundred miles right now!

What Dating A Farmer Involves

Driving into the sunset

The farmer may work long hours, particularly at certain times of the year such as during the calving season or when bringing in the harvest, but there's plenty of scope for spending lots of time together. Much of it may involve sitting on the relatively comfy passenger seat on his tractor as he works late.

As the sun sets over the horizon and you gaze at a meadow of grass swards or a pale golden field that is now bare of wheat, straw or silage, you can congratulate yourselves on a job well done. Driving towards a red ball of fire on the horizon brings a whole new meaning to driving off into the sunset together (except you have to turn around at the ditch when you are on a tractor!)

Making confetti

Do you like the idea of sustainable living? What could be more romantic than plucking chickens together – all those white feathers almost like confetti in the air?

Romance in the fields

Picnics in the field can be a regular occurrence on the farm especially if it is fragmented and many fields are some distance from the farmhouse. To save him the journey time of coming back to the house on foot or on the tractor, you bring his dinner to where he is working. What could be nicer than sitting on a grassy field or a stubbly corn field, using the tractor tyre as a backrest as you gaze at the beautiful countryside?

Even if you are multi-tasking, measuring grass or putting up temporary fencing, a walk across the fields together can bring romance when the sun is shining.

Bringing life into the world

There is nothing more special than bringing life into this world, especially if all is well after a tough birth. Watching a newborn lamb, calf or goat kid struggle on shaky legs to its mother's udder makes it all worthwhile. If it is one of the first births you have witnessed, you may even have the privilege of naming the new little creature. Then you can always keep an eye out for it in the herd.

When I was about seventeen, I was going out with a non-farmer and we were babysitting my younger brother and keeping an eye on a cow calving at the same time. We were getting a bit anxious about the cow. The feet and nose had been protruding for a long time but she wasn't making much progress, so we eventually decided to put a rope on the calf's feet and pulled it out. My father was very impressed and gave me the bull calf. I didn't name it after the boyfriend!

Tender toughness

He may look a little rough around the edges, and he may sound gruff when he's shouting at cattle or trying to move some stubborn sheep. But just watch those huge gnarled red hands, with their calluses, welts and non-manicured nails, become tender when he picks up a newborn lamb to bring it to the warmth of the shed or kitchen. You know it isn't the value of the lamb that he is thinking about when he is trying to keep it alive. It is about not wanting to see new life ebb away and giving the newborn a chance to enjoy life and gambol in the sunshine. Most farmers have a very tender streak when it comes to newborns and will spend hours trying to keep sickly ones alive.

Life and death on the farm

He may not be the most reliable and might cancel dates at the last minute or turn up two hours late. It becomes a fact of life in farming, because if an animal is sick, it becomes top priority (as long as everyone in the family is healthy of course). There is an expression among farmers when there is death on the farm "as long as it happens outside the house", meaning that they will get over an animal's death if the family is healthy. Another common saying is "where there's livestock, there's dead stock". Even though farmers are somewhat accustomed to death, losing an animal can take a day or two to recover from when they have fought to keep an animal alive.

Therefore, if he is waiting for the vet or has to stay up to keep checking on a sick animal or a calving cow, he will not be going anywhere. If the harvest has to be brought in and there is rain looming; he will work through the night and all the next day if necessary. On the other hand, there are farmers that will see some jobs as crucial whereas in reality they can wait. If he rings and says he has to spread farmyard manure and cannot escort you to your friend's wedding, you need to look for another farmer (or someone from another profession) who will put you first.

Celebrate your achievements

Spending a day working together on the farm can be physically exhausting – all that exercise and fresh air for one thing. There is very little to match the satisfaction of finishing a hard day's work, completing tough tasks and being able to hug after a job well done together. As a wise old man once told me, it is important to celebrate the achievements of hard work before you rush on to the next job or challenge, so make the celebrations fun and memorable.

Farming Knowledge You Will Acquire Quickly

Long before you marry your farmer, you will be called upon to help out on the farm. You may be broken in gently or the farming training might be more volatile, depending on the season, his patience levels and the urgency of the situation. If your intended is a livestock farmer, working with animals has the benefits of helping you get close to nature, enjoy a workout and spend quality time with your beloved. It may also lead to your first strong argument and one of you storming off into the sunset.

Sorting cattle

Sorting animals on livestock farms is a job that has to be done fairly often. It means dividing a batch of calves, cattle, cows, sheep, goats or whatever animals you have into two groups. Calves are divided according to size or sex. Older cattle are divided according to size or pregnancy status. Sheep may be divided according to how many lambs they are carrying, as ewes pregnant with twins or triplets will require more feeding than mothers of single lambs. Lambs and calves are separated from their mothers at the weaning stage.

How it works is the animals are brought into the yard and one person (usually you) stands by a gate. It is your job to allow selected animals to pass through the gate to a new group and stop any sly chancers getting past you and the gateway. The farmer tries to sort through the animals and select the right ones to drive up towards you, but that is not always possible. Sometimes a number of right and wrong ones come together and it is your job to understand the shouted instructions and act accordingly. You do not have much time to interpret his yells and gestures. Telepathy and a good understanding of your farmer's meaning are imperative. Never take offence if curses are hurled at you.

Sorting animals can be fraught. If they are not accustomed to you, they are even more uneasy and flighty. The younger the animal, the more erratic they tend to be. If the concrete ground is mucky and wet, they treat it like a skating rink and skid towards you. If they aren't used to being handled and are over a year old, it can be a little hair-raising trying to separate the two or three creatures coming towards you. Yearling cattle are big animals and it can feel as though they are heading straight for you, veering to the side in the nick of time. It is yet to happen that one crashes into this farmerette, but you never know.

The farmer knows his stock so well; he can tell you the dam (mother) of each one, which ones have the same sire (father) and which are the males and females, without having to look between their legs. To you, there is very little difference in their appearance. Friesian cattle are usually black and white. According to any farmer, it is easy to tell them apart as their markings can differ significantly. For the uninitiated though, they look remarkably similar. Breeds such as Aberdeen Angus (black all over), Limousins (dark red all over), Herefords (red with white heads), or Charolais (creamy white) are even harder to tell apart as their colouring are very alike. Heaven help you if he has one of these herds.

You must remember that no matter where you stand, you will never be in the right place. There actually isn't a right place unless you can clone yourself half a dozen times but there is no point telling the farmer that either, just resign yourself and shrug.

How to decipher those shouted instructions

Determining difference by colour.

Having "the BLACK ONE" hollered at you does not make it clear if the blackest animal is to be let through the gate or turned back into the group, so establish this before you start!

Note that "the black one" does not mean that the animal is all black. It simply means that it has slightly more black on its coat than its comrades. The same goes for "the white one"! Having an occasional red and white animal is handy as they are easily identified. I always note their presence in our Friesian herd with a sigh of relief.

Determining difference by stick.

If the animals look very similar, instructions may be reduced to "THAT one, get 'THAT one". The trick is to be able to look at the direction the stick is pointing along the same line as the farmer, so you can see exactly which of the three cattle he is pointing at. This is impossible. You are standing in the gateway, so you are doomed before you start.

Determining difference by sex.

"The bull, let the bull in" doesn't help when there are three calves' heads coming towards you and you can't see between their legs.

Determining difference by size.

When the farmer shouts "the BIGGEST ONE," you must learn to tell the difference in size between calves. If they are standing together, there may be only a couple of inches in the difference in height or girth. When they are running, it is nigh impossible to tell. However, to the farmer who knows them well, the difference seems obvious.

Eyes in the Back of your Head

Having eyes in the back of your head is handy too. While you are focusing on the three calves coming towards you and trying to work out which is the blackest, the biggest and the male, an opportunist calf might try to scoot in behind you. If that situation occurs and two calves run into the wrong group, it is a good idea to remember these four things:

- It is never your fault; the cattle are on edge seeing a strange person anyway.
- It is not the end of the world; they can always be retrieved.
- Your mother told you never to swear in public.
- Retain your composure; losing it will not help the situation.

What is likely to happen is that your body and brain battle each other as you try to decide whether to run after the wayward cattle or stay in position and prevent others following them. Or you may just leave for home as you hear the farmer's curses coming in your direction. As a result, you

end up doing a strange kind of hoppity dance, with arms and legs flailing – a long shriek may be emitted from your mouth too. This will be incomprehensible to man and beast. The farmer views it all as your fault. You lose your temper and shout back, including some swear words for good measure. How the hell were you supposed to know that the black one was blacker on the other side anyway?

If a wayward one does escape, the hoppity dance is not all negative. It might even ease the tension and you end up having a good laugh about it all. After all, you must both appreciate that any bad language hurled at each other while sorting animals will be forgotten once the job is completed. Sorting stock can be a fraught experience and bad language is almost expected. Hurling swear words at each other can be almost enjoyable – as at what other time can you tell your loved one he is a blethering idiot for not realising you are not telepathic? The important thing is to realise that it will only get worse once you do get married. If you do fall out over sorting cattle, there is the fun of making up later on. We usually say "I love you" at the start of such tasks, knowing it could be a few hours before we say it again!

The Sheep Situation

Sheep are sometimes depicted as rather silly animals who will follow each other no matter what else is going on. Once a lone sheep decides to go for a stroll through a gap in the hedge or an open gate, it won't be long before the others think it is a good idea too.

Sheep can be stubborn and a law onto themselves. If a group of sheep decide that they do not want to go through an open gate, they stand in a mass in the field and refuse to move. If the ground at the open gate is mucky, you will probably need more than the rattle from a bucket of sweet tasting nuts to persuade them. Most farmers have a good sheepdog. If he does not, buy him one for his next birthday. This is a little like him buying you lingerie so he can enjoy you wearing it – you buy him the dog so it can do the running and endure the shouting while you have a rest.

There is quite a lot of work involved in sheep farming, between scanning (checking to see how many lambs the ewes are carrying), dosing, dipping, tagging, dagging and shearing,. They all need to caught quite a few times during the year. You could be the person doing the catching and the holding of the sheep, which can be trickier than it looks. It might just happen that a sheep takes you unawares. If this happens, the sheep just might fit between your legs and carry you down the lane. You will sit there, your legs straddling a strong sheep, unable to get off. Meanwhile, your beloved can scarcely come to help you as he is laughing so much.

What happens when cattle break out

Are you planning a day or evening away from the farm? If a couple of recalcitrant animals are going to find a hole in a fence, they will find it on the evening you are just about to step into your black dress. The telephone will ring and it will be a grumpy neighbour saying he just spotted your cattle. If they are in his grass field, the news isn't too bad. However, if they are in a corn field or have broken out onto the road, it is a very different scenario and they will need to be retrieved as quickly as possible. It means casting that black dress aside and reaching for the jeans and wellies again.

If one or more of your animals are mixed with the other farmer's stock, it can be a headache. It is not too bad if there is a yard nearby where you can separate them, but if there is a lone animal, you may have the task of getting it back out through that gap in the hedge. Even if you are an Olympic sprinter, you will still never run fast enough (in the farmer's opinion) when racing across a field after a stray animal. You will almost have the animal separated from the others when it will become spooked and dash past you again. As you mutter curses under your breath (not aloud as you don't have the breath to do so) you will hear curses being shouted at you to get a move on and run!

The animal is just at the gap; it is just about to walk through that hole in the hedge, looking at the other field as if to say "I recognise you, but the grass is greener on this side?" You are edging towards it with bated breath. Both of you are holding out your arms to give the impression you are a solid wall the calf will not be able to get through, that its only option is to go through that gap, when it suddenly wheels around and starts to run, you gasp and grab at a leg or an ear and feel fresh air whizz by as the animal races off. By this time, you are both so tired and fed up that you can't even swear at each other, knowing you are both doing what you can.

There is a Murphy's law aspect with this – just when you are about to give up and leave the calf there for another day while you come up with a Plan B, it suddenly calms down and walks through the gap as if to say "why didn't you ask me to do this before?".

We rarely get away for a night out, but one night when the children were away on a Beaver camp, we planned to go to the late night cinema. It was nearing ten o'clock when the telephone rang. A neighbour had been piling earth

Would you Marry a Farmer?

beside a fence separating his garden and a field on our outfarm. He had scoffed when we told him the fence had become ineffective as a barrier. As cattle do, they chose to go walkabout on the evening we intended going out. As the seemingly docile cattle casually walking around his garden were actually yearling bulls, we decided we should go over with the dog and make sure they all got back into their rightful field. The neighbour sorted the fence out properly the following day – he was not going to risk another encounter with Friesian bulls.

The farmer knows he won't be flavour of the month if he is phoning with an emergency scenario when you are dressed up to go out. He might think that calling you when you are in old gardening clothes is perfectly fine. You might think it is okay too. However, you might find that the old gardening clothes are not "running after cattle" friendly. The jeans needs a belt or you are wearing an old bra that might not offer you the support required for rounding up cattle. It is hard to run fast when you are trying to hold up your trousers or your boobs!

You might ask "do I need wellies" and you are told "no, it's dry" or "no, you just need to stop them". ALWAYS WEAR WELLIES - there will be muck, there will be cowpats, and there will be long wet grass.

Moving bulls

Bulls are male bovines that have not been castrated. Bulls were traditionally kept for breeding purposes. One or two bulls were used by farmers to inseminate all their cows and heifers, depending on the size of the herd. A bull can "cover" (inseminate) about 40 cows in a season. Many farmers are now fattening the males as bulls rather than as castrated steers, as bulls thrive more efficiently and can be slaughtered earlier. The disadvantage is bulls can be dangerous, with Friesian bulls being much more aggressive than beef breeds. Handling them until they are sold at 16-24 months needs to be done with caution.

Safety is a huge issue on all farms and it is too easy to think that a bull is just another bovine. They are a temperamental, towering mass of testosterone-charged muscle and bone. They are unpredictable, strong and ruthless. Moving bulls is a dangerous task – never ever belittle the dangers. Having a good cattle dog is imperative but it can only do so much.

This is how the process tends to work when bulls are moved from one field to another or brought into the shed. The dog is sent into the field to bring out the bulls. You, the farmerette, stands in a gap to ensure the bulls go in the right direction, perhaps behind a barrier such as a tractor or a gate. You are gripping a pitchfork and wondering how fast you can reach the other side of the fence if necessary.

You know the danger is very real when the usually complacent farmer leaves the door to the tractor open and casually mentions that you can always jump up the three high steps into it should the need arise! Telling you that the electric wire isn't on so you can dash for it without the worry of being mildly electrocuted is not overly reassuring – the bulls won't be stung by the electric current either.

If the bulls pause to look at you, this is normal. After all, you are a strange being in their midst and they are naturally curious creatures. You only need to worry if they start bellowing, lowering their heads or pawing the ground with their hooves. To encourage them to move on, wave the pitchfork, hop up and down to make yourself look as large as possible and shout some nonsensical words. No one but the farmer, the dog and the bulls will see you dancing your strange jig, so you won't look too much of a fool – though at least you should be a safe fool.

Dairy Cows

Dairy cows need to be milked twice a day. Some farmers milk once a day, others milk three times but the general consensus on Irish farms is for twice a day. Cows calve in the spring on most dairy farms. They are milked for ten months of the year and "go dry" for approximately two months before they calve again. On "liquid milk" farms (which are contracted to provide milk 365 days a year), they will have autumn and spring calving herds, so there is never a dry spell.[59] The "liquid milk" farmer never gets a break from milking.

It means that full days off are rare for a dairy farmer unless he has a good workman or reliable relief milker. The Sunday evening milking still has to be done, no matter what the occasion.

Bringing in the cows is one of the nicest jobs on a dairy farm. The cows know the routine. If you enter their field at any other time during the day and stand still in their midst, they amble up to you after a couple of minutes to sniff and lick at you. Enter the field in the evening or early morning and they know it is milking time. A couple of eager "leaders" start to move towards the gate while others chew their cud once more before getting to their feet. If they have been lying for some time, they need to relieve their bladders and yes, cows wee for ages. In the spring, they are keen to get into the parlour as their udders are filled to bursting point and are uncomfortable (in the early days after calving). In the autumn when the nights are shorter, they prefer to eat more during the day and chew their cud at night. Therefore, their bellies are full, udders not so full and they feel lazy about moving, particularly if there is an uphill climb to the milking parlour.

White clouds break up the blue sky as you walk through pale green grass bitten off short. Dark green patches highlight the presence of cowpats. You can take the time to appreciate the beauty of the scenery and the changing colours of the landscape and the sky. There are always two or three cows at the far end of the field that refuse to move until you or the dog goes up to them. Sod's law will play a part here as one of those is always lame and makes slow progress across the field. If it is late summer, midges whirr around, the cows' tails whisk from side to side and your hat will keep the flies somewhat at bay. Cows walk at a pace that is leisurely and relaxing, and getting into their zone is calming too.

From the age of nine, I used to bring in the cows to be milked in the evenings. I viewed it as my job; I enjoyed the solitude, the strolling along behind the ambling cows. The only problem was our cattle dog who was absolutely useless. He would occasionally take it into his head to come along for the cows and chase them across the field. We have heavy land and if it had been a wet summer, the dog was not popular and nor was I, because I hadn't been able to control him and prevent the cows turning grass to mucky deep hoofprints.

I have a terrible sense of direction. I still get confused in my local town regarding the one way system and have to ask our eleven year old son for directions sometimes. Once when I was going for the cows with my dad at the age of eight, I recall his exclamation of annoyance as most of the cows decided to head for home the "long way around" via a hill. One lame old lady continued to plod along the path though.

"You bring that cow home," he said as he headed off over the hill.

"But I don't know the way," was my alarmed response, as I imagined myself getting lost with an old cow.

"Follow the cow, she knows the way," he called back.

I dutifully followed the lame cow home and marvelled that a cow could be so clever to know the way home on her own, particularly when we were probably the same age!

I still enjoy going for the cows; it is one of my favourite jobs on the farm, though I am still not trusted with monitoring for cows being on heat when I am bringing them in. There are all sorts of signs to look for, such as a cow being extra alert, with pricked ears, acting slightly flightily, bellowing, passing mucus, jumping on another cow or standing still while another cow jumps on her. The only ones I pick up on are the jumping and standing ones!

I help my farmer in the milking parlour when he is milk recording. We nearly murdered each other the first time. The meters wouldn't read some of the bar codes which caused delays. I became confused as to which cows had been sampled. I was in the way, my beloved was impatient, and the raised voices were making the cows nervous, which meant that they were excreting with vigour, force and a good aim. That didn't exactly lighten the mood. We have a herringbone parlour, which means the pit floor is about three feet lower than the cows – our heads are just under the cows' tails! Hence, we have to keep a watchful eye to avoid getting splattered with muck. For the second milk recording, we hugged beforehand and took everything more calmly. We worked in synchronicity as we ducked and dived between the jars and the clusters in our ten-unit parlour. Apart from the cow that excretes with such immense force she can drive it across the parlour at full speed and with good aim, the cows, man and woman all worked in perfect harmony.

Stopping a gap

Occasionally cattle have to be moved along the road from one field to another. It is commonly thought that narrow country roads are seldom travelled by cars but once you are thinking of bringing cattle out, they become busy thoroughfares. "Stopping a gap" is the term given to preventing cattle or sheep going into a house entrance, another field, a side road or a gap in the hedge.

The farmer is in the field with the dog trying to round up the cattle, get them to the gateway and out on the road. It is your job to stop any traffic once the cattle are close to the gate. You wave down the first car to slow it down and crane your neck to see if the cattle are close to the exit. You know that if you let the car on, the cattle will come running out of the field and be spooked by the car. You also know that if you tell the driver to wait, it will take your beloved and the dog about ten minutes to round up the cattle and get them out. You explain the situation; the person says they will drive slowly. You wait with bated breath until the car has passed the gate.

If the cars have to queue up for a few minutes, it invariably happens that one occupant becomes impatient and starts to edge their car out just as the cattle are approaching the gate. Looking assertive in a checked shirt with shoulders back and raising a pitchfork higher into the air communicates the message that you are not to be messed with and the car should sidle back into position again. If necessary, growl "Stay there" while lifting the pitchfork. It is a very brave driver who would dare argue. When it is time for them to move on, a wave, a smile and a "thank you" reassures them that you are not always a crazy country bumpkin.

It can also happen that you have the job of "stopping a gap" along the road to ensure that the moving cattle or sheep do not detour into somebody's garden. Stopping a gap can be interpreted as having to block two or three gateways that are quite close together. Mercifully, the temporary wealth of the Celtic Tiger era means many new houses have huge electric gates that stay closed, except when the occupants and their visitors drive in or out. If the houses do not have gates at all, you have the choice of dancing the length of the three driveways to ensure none of your cattle enter or seeing if any of the houses has an occupant who is free to stand in their own driveway. It is likely that an elderly person will emerge, either delighted with the distraction or grumpy because they were in the middle of watching the *Emmerdale* omnibus. You then wonder if it was such a good idea - will he be capable of stopping a yearling as he stands looking rather crotchety in the middle of his gateway? The cattle either race by, too fast to give him a second glance, or they rush up and stop abruptly, bemused by this strange person who is waving his walking stick at them. For a split second, it looks like they just might hop over the opposite hedge into the neighbouring field.

Moving cattle to the out farm two miles away was an annual event when I was a child. We looked forward to the excitement of it – although it was planned with military precision and everyone knew which gap they had to stop, we never quite knew what might happen. There would be certain points where one or two of us would have to stop a gap and then run or cycle past the cattle on the narrow road, in time to reach the next gap before the cattle did. Sometimes it seemed as if a couple of animals were just about to jump an inadequate fence into one of the neighbour's fields. Thankfully, that rarely happened. We now move them to and fro in a cattle trailer, due to increased traffic and less manpower and for safety reasons.

Stopping a gap isn't for the faint hearted farmerette. Ensure that the farmer has the cattle trained to recognise that a strand of electric wire tied across a gateway just might sting the life out of them – stopping those gaps will be a lot easier! It offers very similar results to cloning oneself.

How to herd

Herding cattle should be pretty easy, shouldn't it? After all, it is just a case of counting the cattle or sheep in a field, making sure they are all there, fit and healthy. It is very easy as long as there are less than fifty, they are not all bunched up together and they do not view you as the latest curiosity.

What the farmer tends to forget is that the cattle are accustomed to him. He can arrive in the field and saunter amongst them and they do not bat an eyelid. If they are lying down contented, chewing their cud, he can tell if an animal appears off-form and the herding is finished in a matter of minutes. When you arrive in the field however, it is a very different story. If they are lying down, count them first. Once they are moving around, it is much more difficult. You can then get them up and moving to ensure they all look healthy.

If one stays lying down, do not presume the worst and call the vet. Once they get the call that an animal is down, they tend to drop whatever else they are doing and rush out. You are going to be standing there with egg on your face if the animal gets up in the meantime and you discover it was just lazy! Occasionally an animal will not get up until you go nearer to it – maybe it was in a world of its own, maybe it has a sore foot and cannot be bothered, or perhaps it is a lazy, stubborn fecker.

Counting animals from a distance can be quite a challenge. You are trying to work out if there are three or four animals in that little group and if a leg belongs to another animal or not. It is one thing to count seventy animals that are stationary, but when half of them are moving towards you to see what you are, it is quite another matter. It is also tricky if it is a wet day and they are all huddled close together beside the ditch.

Bovines are naturally inquisitive, friendly and curious creatures. If you are standing still, looking slightly puzzled, have your finger in the air and appear to be counting away to yourself, they are going to come over to check you out. They will look at each other and snigger as if to say "Look, it's her again, he sent her over to count us, ha, let's confuse her." Then they will huddle in together or walk quickly in a mass towards you, impossible to count in one condensed batch.

If you stand still, the cattle come up to sniff at you and exhale their grassy breaths over you. They sneak out a long tongue to give your clothes and wellies a lick, and they nudge you with their heads. If you swat at them, they step back for a moment and then come back for more. As you turn to walk back to the gate, they follow you, so close that you wonder if their heads might butt you in the back and knock you over. It can feel slightly threatening to have dozens of large animals lumbering behind you, each weighing in excess of 350kgs. Although they are vegetarian, you cannot help but wonder if they might be thinking of taking a bite out of you.

When you are herding, do not enter the same field as yearling bulls on your own under any circumstances. You herd them from the other side of the hedge. You simply count to the best of your ability to make sure they are all there. The farmer can check them more closely when he has the tractor and dog with him. Suckler cows with calves at foot can be equally dangerous. Do not bring a dog into the field with you, as cows will immediately go on the defensive and attack the dog to protect their calves. If they see you as a threat, they may suddenly decide to attack you. People have been as seriously injured by suckler cows as by bulls.

Herding sheep can also have its ups and downs. They certainly all look the same – balls of off-white or off-black wool. However, being smaller in size can make them easier to count. At particular times of the year, when heavily in lamb or before they are shorn, sheep can roll onto their backs and are unable to right themselves. Unless a human is there with a helping hand, they can die quite quickly. It means grabbing the sheep by her woolly coat, avoiding her kicking legs and giving her a good tug or push to right her. She then gives you an ungrateful glare before trotting off to join the rest of the flock.

Herding is one of the nicest jobs on the farm. An essential daily task, you can multi-task and enjoy your daily exercise with a bracing walk on windy days, or you can loiter and pick wild flowers or blackberries. The scent of wild honeysuckle as you wander along is almost impossible to beat on a summer's evening.

Becoming a midwife

As a livestock farmer, no matter how many times you see animals being born, there is still something very special in watching a new mother turn around to see what she has delivered and start to lick it all over. Their maternal instinct of knowing what they have to do is incredible. To see a tiny newborn wriggle onto its feet and lurch towards the udder for a first feed is also a beautiful sight, and you will never tire of it.

Most of us think of newborns (human or animal) as healthy, warm, dry, clean, cuddly and hopefully relatively quiet. The reality can sometimes be very different on a farm, whatever about a maternity hospital. Apparently many farmers used to look for a nurse or teacher when looking for a wife, not just for the pay packet but for the midwifery skills in a nurse!

Maybe you expressed an interest in nursing when you were a child but when you felt sick at the sight of blood; you decided it was not going to be the right career choice. I thought about it at one point but decided that I just didn't have the right bedside manner for sick people, being of a matter-of-fact, unsympathetic and practical nature.

The good news is there isn't too much blood when assisting at the birth of a calf or lamb. Many cows and sheep give birth without any intervention at all. They just need checks during the labour that all is going to plan, without disturbing them unnecessarily. However, there are always some that present problems and you might be the main assistant, so it is best to know what is going to be expected of you.

Farmers tend to be impatient if a cow takes a long time about calving, particularly if it is at night and they want to go to bed. My husband calls it "eejiting around" I always respond by saying that I am sure the cow would prefer for the calf to be born, rather than enduring contractions every few minutes. An older cow that takes her time, particularly if the calf turns out to be small, is always be referred to as "a lazy auld hoor". I often wonder if midwives and obstetricians speak of labouring women in the same way in the staff rooms of maternity hospitals.

Complications can arise if a calf is breech (comes backwards – the head should be coming first) or if it is lying on its back in the womb and needs to be turned. If it is a big calf, the cow may need more than a helping hand delivering. If a ewe or goat is expecting three or four offspring, their legs can all be tangled up, or the first one might be the largest and is blocking the way for the others who are also trying to get out.

Farmers use a calving jack or a pulley to help deliver a calf if it is proving difficult. A rope is tied to the calf's feet and pressure is put on the rope using the pulley to gently guide the calf out. The farmer has his hand at the cow ensuring the calf is coming the right way, and you are at the 'pulley' end. The good news is this is about a metre away from the cow! Once everything is ready, you are told how many times to "work" the pulley (with occasional shrieks for "stop" or "quick, once more") and all going well, the calf slides out.

A couple of years ago, a cow was delivering twins and the one coming first was breech and needed to be pulled out backwards. Breech births are higher risk as if the umbilical cord breaks and the calf gets stuck on the way out, the result would be death or brain damage. My farmer was trying to get hold of the tail in case it twisted backwards and impeded the delivery. He couldn't find the tail anywhere! He could feel lots of legs and he knew it was twins. He knew he had two back legs belonging to one calf, but he just could not find the tail. In the end, we pulled and it came out fine, as did its twin sister a few minutes later. It was the first time we had ever seen a calf with no tail. It had not been pulled off! For some reason, it just did not form.

If it has been a long and difficult labour, it can be a bit "touch and go" and the calf may need some assistance to start breathing. The most effective way to drain mucus from its lungs is to lift it by its wet, mucus covered, blood splattered back legs and pull them over a gate or the crush rails so its head hangs downwards. You hold onto its legs so it does not slip back, while the farmer massages the area over the lungs and tickles its nose with a bit of straw to stimulate it to breathe. There is no time to be squeamish or wish you had worn gloves. This is very much a two person job, as some newborn calves can be heavy.

It can happen that mouth to mouth resuscitation for the baby calf is needed. Calves are removed from their dairy mothers but depending on the time of birth, they can be with them for a few hours. One evening, my farmer entered the maternity shed to find a cow lying on her calf and smothering it. Getting her up as quickly as he could, he discovered that the calf was not breathing and gave it mouth to mouth resuscitation which worked. The calf went on to enter the dairy herd and produce her own calves. And no, I didn't kiss him for a while!

The birth of lambs and goat kids does not involve heavy lifting but it can be tricky enough untangling limbs. Be warned, because if you show a talent for this, you will end up being the main lambing obstetrician. Every single birth is wonderful, no matter how many you witness, but there are ones that are extra special and will always hold a special place in your heart.

Essential equipment for a livestock farm

Wellies
Stick
Pitchfork
Telepathy
Patience
Composure
Eyes in back of head
Good bra – ideally a sports bra
Good cattle dog
No qualms or fears about looking like an idiot
Forward planning
Ability to run fast and jump over a wire or gate
Belt or baling twine to keep trousers up!

There will be no sympathy if:

A nail breaks
Drizzle turns your hair frizzy
You twist an ankle
A splatter of cow muck ends up in your mouth
Your best jeans get ruined
You fall over
You get soaked

City Girl Meets Country Boy
Are You Incompatible?

If you are from a non farming background, there may be plenty of ways in which you and the farmer are incompatible. That does not mean that it will not work as a relationship. Ensuring that you know about each other's habits, shortfalls, likes and dislikes in advance will prevent angst and will increase your surprise and delight as you become more alike in time. Time will tell whether he becomes more like you or you become the type that has wellies welded to her legs!

Social life

Living in the countryside means that a farmer's social life is probably much tamer than yours. He considers a good night out to be an evening in the pub chatting about farming, whereas you might be more sociable and prefer to go nightclubbing. He is up at 6am to milk the cows, so bopping around until 3am every Saturday night may die a death after marriage. It is too loud at nightclubs to discuss farming, so he doesn't see them as the place to catch up on the news. When you get to the stage that you both enjoy a night in front of the TV with a glass of wine or tea and chocolate, that is heaven!

Pets

A farmer is unlikely to have a high opinion of cats being "mollycoddled" and kept in the house. As far as he is concerned, cats are only good for killing vermin on the farm. If they are to get food at all, it is only enough to keep them alive. Too much food might make them lazy and prevent them from doing their "farm work". If you have a pet cat, do not expect it to receive favourable treatment. If a cat is relatively active in the vermin killing game, it earns more respect from the farmer.

To a farmer, a proper dog must earn its keep by being efficient on the farm, not be afraid of muck, and be capable of rounding up sheep, cows or cattle. It is clipped once a year in hot weather and might be hosed down with the milking parlour hose once in a blue moon. It eats its dinner of leftovers out of a disused biscuit tin. Why a dog should need a silver plated engraved dog bowl, a bejewelled collar, regular trips to be groomed and dog obedience classes always remains a mystery to the farmer. If you have a tiny dog that is carried around in a handbag, the farmer will not want to be seen in your company when carrying the dog. Having a "manly" dog like a Labrador that sleeps in the kitchen is a good middle ground.

It is rare that we have to bring our dog to the vet, but when we saw him looking concussed one day, we rang the small animal vet to ask his advice, as we hadn't noticed him being kicked by one of the cattle. He advised us to bring him in to be checked for meningitis. The dog had been running around in muck for weeks, so it was a case of cutting off the worst of the filthy "dreadlocks" and washing his legs in warm water before putting him in the boot. The vet had to help me lift him up onto the table and as he gingerly took hold of two of his paws, he commented "He's not very clean, is he"? All I could do was reply "He's a lot cleaner than he was an hour ago".

Dinner

They say that the way to a man's heart is through his stomach. That is certainly true of a farmer. After all, the fact he is a fine strapping lad is no trick of nature. The Irish Mammy is celebrated for her wholesome cooking. For years, he has eaten porridge for breakfast to keep the cold out. His dinner has traditionally been meat, two vegetables, gravy and what looks like a ton of floury potatoes, followed by a home baked pudding. His tea might be a good fry-up.

If you are a domestic goddess and like good plain wholesome food, you will be in heaven cooking for this man, who loves his food. If you detest cooking or prefer lighter meals such as pasta or rice, you are going to have to find a middle ground. The best option might be to have your sandwich lunch at work and he continues to have his spud and meat dinner with his mammy. You can both have a fajita, pasta or rice dinner in the evening. Young farmers can eat two dinners each day without any problem and not gain an ounce.

Holidays

The best thing about being self employed is you are your own boss and you don't have to answer to anyone when you want to take a holiday or a day off. To anyone apart from the livestock of course! There are ways to ensure you are both happy even if you have completely different tastes in holidays. If you like beautiful historic houses and gardens, choose ones with adjoining farms and parkland. Once he can see some sheep or cows, he is happy.

If you are driving through a town and you would like to do some shopping, see if the local mart is on. He can pop in and "see what the trade is like" and you can then go clothes shopping to your heart's content.

Shopping

It can take a while to get used to the fact you are living some distance from the nearest shop. Running out of butter means that you are prepared to jump into the car, perhaps momentarily forgetting that it takes you twenty minutes to get there. He does not see a problem in doing without it until the next grocery shop. Or you get the response "sure isn't there plenty of milk in the tank, can't you make some butter"? Once you start making scones and clotted cream for visitors, you know you have become a rural domestic goddess.

I am a disorganised shopper, hence I frequently run out of key ingredients such as bread (sandwiches for school lunches) or essentials such as dishwasher tablets. Although the local shop is only a mile away, I rarely jump into the car to go and get a single item. I have worked out how much washing up liquid to add to the dishwasher to get it to work reasonably well and as long as I have crackers for school lunches and flour and milk to make pancakes or bread, we don't starve.

The Goldfish Bowl

One of the biggest adjustments of moving from the town to the country is realising the limited nature of the goldfish bowl that is the country parish. Next is realising that you are often the biggest goldfish in the bowl, as you have the most novelty value. Do not think that you can do anything that will not be noticed. If you normally leave the house at 8am, and change that time one morning to 8:15 am, it will be noticed and commented on as the neighbours muse over what might have caused you to leave fifteen minutes later.

I love the isolation of living on a farm that is some distance from the main road. We live on a hill and can see for miles yet don't have any close neighbours. I love that my space is my own, that nobody can see in my living room window. I can leave the curtains open day and evening if I wish, and I can run up the yard in my pyjamas for milk and there is no one to see me (unless I scare an early morning sales rep). Rather than hearing neighbours talking or children shouting, I hear birds singing and cows mooing. Instead of hearing cars on the road, I hear the occasional trundle of the tractor or the loader.

Living in apparent isolation on a farm does not necessarily result in loneliness. Most farmer families tend to be involved in various communities – the local parish, the school, the GAA or local charities. People give you space to let you decide what groups you want to join and once you do decide, you will be welcomed with open arms. If an unhappy event occurs, such as an accident, the community support is extensive and wholehearted.

What can take time to get used to is the fact that everyone knows everyone and everything is of interest to everyone. News is not what is happening on the world stage, with the latest election results or a recent bomb explosion in another country. News is who is getting married, who is pregnant, who had a baby, who sowed barley this year, who is re-seeding, who has their cows out first, who has good grass growth, who has cut their silage already, who is milking late, what price a farmer got for his cattle at the mart, who has been buying a lot of new clothes lately and what bid is on a local field for sale. By the way, if you happen to stroll down a lane and go for a walk across said field, it will travel like wildfire that you are thinking of buying that exact field.

People tend to make presumptions about your activities or make up their own stories. If you are seen at the local shop at a different time than usual, filling your car with diesel and wearing a black coat, it might be presumed that you are going to a funeral. Some neighbours may then spend time looking up the death notices to work out which funeral it might be. For farmhouses on relatively quiet roads, the occasional vehicle passing provides an endless source of conversation, particularly if it is a strange tractor. Which contractor was driving it? What was in the trailer? Did it look like a heavy load? Which farmer was he working for last? Where might he be going to next? Did he have a passenger? Wasn't he driving fast?

If you have moved into the farmhouse, any alterations and decorating you do becomes news. There may also be some discussion about your pregnant or non-pregnant status. If you have news that would be deemed to be shocking or larger than life, be assured that although your ears might burn red hot for at least a week, something else will always come along. If you bought land, that lasts about twenty minutes. If you reveal you were married before, that might last a few days. If you disclose you are in a same sex relationship, the gossip might last a few days too.

However, it all becomes old news sooner or later, until the next victim of village gossip comes along.

10 signs you will make a great farmer's wife

1. You are strong and see heavy lifting as a challenge to be achieved.
2. Wearing wellies in dirty conditions makes you as happy as a pig in muck.
3. You get more satisfaction from washing calf buckets than manicuring your nails.
4. Feeding calves late at night because there was an emergency Caesarean section is seen as one of those things.
5. You have a really efficient filing system so you know exactly where every single piece of potentially important paper is at any time.
6. You are able to whip up a batch of scones and cups of tea at a moment's notice.
7. You are able to shower, change and apply make-up in ten minutes. You might have stepped in the back door in wellies at 8:30, but you are able to walk out the front door in high heels before 9:00.
8. You know the names of the different types of tractors and get almost as excited as a three year old boy when you see particularly big models – you will be a great mum too.
9. You can drive a huge vehicle at a moment's notice without gulping in fear.
10. You can multitask.

10 signs he will make a good farming husband

1. He can multi-task relatively well, especially if it is child minding while driving a tractor.
2. He can throw a meal together even if it is just bacon, sausage and egg.
3. He is a good mechanic and good at problem solving, which saves a lot of money when machinery breaks down.
4. He can detect danger at a hundred paces – farms are dangerous places
5. The welfare of his animals is important to him. Someone who is kind to animals will always be kind to people.
6. He is patient. Farmers have to be patient with the weather, so if he can turn that patience to his wife and children too, all is good.
7. He is an optimist. Farmers have to be optimistic to be involved in farming. Therefore, no matter how many clouds come along, he always sees a silver lining.
8. He is so accustomed to working with muck; a child's nappy should be a piece of cake.
9. He is capable of surprising you occasionally with a spontaneous night out to make up for all the cancelled evenings out.
10. He can still see the romance in a walk across the fields, or the fun in a race across the hay bales.

For better, for worse ....

Getting married to anyone is a huge decision; there's the "for better, for worse" element of it and you don't want to think about the "for worse". Dating and marrying a farmer makes it an even bigger step, given their hard work ethic and commitment to animals and the land not to mention the often haphazard and fluctuating cashflow situation. Will your life ever resemble what you experienced before? Of course it won't, but at least you will be prepared if you have read these tips. Consider them as the preamble to your "pre-marriage course".

Section 4

Just Married

Do Ewe Take This Man?

Country Living

It can take time to become accustomed to living in the countryside if you have always lived in a town or city. There are lots of differences not related to cows or sheep. Once you fall in love with country living, you will never want to live in an apartment or semi-detached house again, but it does take time to acclimatise. You find that many of your old friends disappear, and while one or two may resurface occasionally when you visit friends in the city, most are gone for good. It may take a little time to make new friends and to get used to them. Think of it as similar to breaking in a new pair of shoes ... or even wellies.

Would you Marry a Farmer?

New friends replace old friends

Old Friends	New Friends
Cappuccinos and skinny lattes.	Pot of tea and big mugs.
Fashionable jeans.	Hardwearing work wear, overalls and denims.
High heels – Jimmy C	Wellies – Dunbar.
Your P60.	The accountant and an annual tax payment.
Your credit card.	Your bank manager. You'll be seeing him or her for the annual loan reviews, so you might as well become friends rather than enemies.
Your personal shopper.	Your farm advisor. It can be hard to think outside the box, but is much easier if you have a good farm advisor.
Your cat.	The cattle dog. A good working dog is a farmer's best friend. If you do not want to be running up and down fields all the time, ensure that the farmer has a good dog which will be worth his weight in gold.
Ready meals or takeaways.	Roast dinners with meat, potatoes and two vegetables.
Your beautician or spa therapist.	The doctor. Men are terrible at going for check-ups. Farmers are the worst. Having a friendly doctor makes it easier.
Your best friend who is a fashion advisor and companion on all nights out.	The Department of Agriculture – okay, not the whole department. Get the name and direct number of one intelligent and helpful soul. This will save you endless hours waiting to reach the right section.

Your store cards.	Overdraft. You can love it or hate it so it is easier if you just accept it as a friend.
Central heating.	Draughty house and open fires/wood stove. Maybe an Aga or Rayburn.
Walks on a town path.	Cross country walks. Even though you live near small country roads, they are too dangerous to walk on, so exercise must be in wellies across the fields.
Spontaneity.	Three months of planning for a single weekend away.
Anonymity – no one knows who you are.	You are the centre of the goldfish bowl that is parish life.
Stroll to the local shop for pint of milk.	Drive three miles to a local shop for milk or don wellies and go up the yard.
2 weeks' holiday abroad every summer.	A few days away while the cows are dry.
The Irish Times, The Gloss, House and Home, Hello and OK magazines.	*The Farmers Journal, Farmers Weekly,* Artificial Insemination catalogues, Agriland.ie (farming news website)
Weekends off.	An occasional day off to go to the Ploughing Match, Dublin Horse Show, the races or an agricultural show ...

Calendar – For Farming Wives

January – Now is your time to get him away on holidays before the lambing or calving starts. Trying to get him to go abroad for at least a week to the sun or the snow can be a challenge though. Skiing might not be a good idea; if he breaks a leg, who will be the one to lamb and calve all those animals?

February – Calving/lambing is starting so you will only see your husband for quick meals and in the maternity ward. Your jobs include washing calf buckets and teat feeders and teaching calves how to drink milk. If you are married to a sheep or goat farmer, your smaller hands may be required occasionally during a difficult labour!

March – is almost the same as February but with more calves to feed. Cows may be sold and your midwifery skills are needed more as the farmer spends more time at the mart. Lambing is in full swing. Tillage farmers are ploughing, tilling and sowing their crops.

April – Reread the section providing tips for "sorting cattle" as they will be needed. The first decent milk cheque of the year arrives and goes out again just as quickly. The sales representatives know exactly what day the milk cheque arrives and form a queue in the yard. The spring sowing continues and early lambs go to the factory.

May – It feels like the calves have only just been born and it is time to get the cows pregnant again. It is artificial insemination season on many farms. Cows and heifers are being watched closely for signs of being on heat, the breeding charts are filled in and pored over at every meal and should you move them from the end of the kitchen table, consternation ensues if he cannot find them. Tillage farmers are spraying and fertilising their crops as weather permits.

June – It is silage time which involves a huge grocery shop on your part and at least one full day of cooking three meals for many hungry men. Between the sheep shearing and the spreading of slurry, it is just as well it all happens around the longest days of the year.

July – Time to spread slurry, improve drainage, reseed fields, harvest winter corn and cut hay. This is when you try and get one day off and head to the beach, to ensure that the children feel like they have had a holiday.

August – It is harvest time, so it is time to cut corn, bale straw, draw straw home for the winter, complete your re-seeding of fields for the year and other tasks. Sheep are monitored for blowfly and it is time for their annual dip. There is an agricultural show on every Sunday so you are spoilt for choice. You need to have worked out when you want your lambs born the following year (using the Easter dates as a guide) so you can time when to put the rams with the ewes.

September – This is the month for the Ploughing Championships and festivals all over the country. If the harvest is in, it is a good month for taking some time off and recharging the batteries before the onslaught of winter. As soon as the children go back to school, the weather usually improves and an Indian summer might even occur. The ploughing and sowing for winter corn commences.

October – Evenings start to draw in and the working day should be somewhat shorter, except for those with winter milking herds, as the cows start to calve. You might be lucky enough to pull the curtains early and sit by the fire while the rain lashes against the window. Maize will be harvested for winter feed. It is also the month for sorting out your tax affairs and working out where you will find the money to pay the Revenue.

November – In spring-calving herds, the cows go "dry" towards the end of the month, so now is the time to draw up the list of jobs you need done in the house, from shelves that need to be hung to rooms that require painting. It is a quiet month for tillage farmers so write him a long list.

December – There is no rest for the wicked and farmers have to do some work on Christmas Day. Many "double fodder" the day before so work is at a minimum. If there are lots of visitors, farmers are known to nip out to feed the animals just to get a break from the constant chat and the heat of the room.

Life with a Farmer

Your domestic god

Being self employed, farmers work long hours, but there are times of the year when they are less busy and that is your time slot for getting him to go on holidays, go on days out and do some work around the house. If he is a dairy farmer and the cows are dry for two months, December and January are your months for making the most of his free time. As he is used to long hours, he won't complain about starting to hang shelves at 6pm. Being accustomed to making repairs on the farm, he should be well able to fix loose skirting boards, rewire plugs, paint the kitchen, strip wallpaper and sweep the chimney. Do remember if the jobs are not done by the time the cows start calving, it will have to wait for another ten months. If he is a good cook, get him baking and cooking during those two months so you can catch up on other work, or pleasures. He might complain that he isn't getting much of a rest so there lies your perfect reason to persuade him to go away for a holiday in January.

You become a chauffeur

When driving anywhere, your sleep-deprived husband (who allegedly works harder and longer hours than you) struggles to stay awake after an average of ten miles. Therefore, you become a chauffeur if you are travelling with him. You drive along in silence with the radio down low, trying to keep the kids from shouting and fighting in the back while he nods away in the passenger seat. He wakes at intervals to marvel at how quickly the journey is going.

Going on holidays or travelling different roads than he normally does means that your farmer husband has lots to entertain him when he wakes up occasionally. Looking over the ditches to see what crops are growing, how they are looking, the varied quality of the grass, if silage has been cut yet, whether the cows look in fine fettle or not – it is all fascinating to a farmer. If he sees something interesting, he perks up to sit higher in the seat so he can see over the hedges. At times, he requests that you slow down so he can have a better look. Your conversations are interrupted by comments like "goodness, they have their cows out already", "wouldn't it be lovely to have a dry farm in Cork", "those cattle could do with feeding up", "that silage is light/heavy", "that's a grand field of sheep", "those straw bales are plentiful" and "how do they expect those calves to thrive on that bit of grass". Intelligent responses are not required, just an acknowledgement that you heard him. A long mmmm will do.

Illness is not recommended

Do not get sick! Once your husband has calved cows and milked for a week while experiencing 'flu, you will never get sympathy again! Flu always seems to occur during the busiest calving fortnight when there really isn't time to get sick. Heavy colds and morning sickness are scoffed at, unless you are so sick you have to be hospitalised. If you are really sick and he eventually does start to take it seriously, you become worried and wonder if he knows something you don't! You must have a reliable and sympathetic member of the family nearby, hire a babysitter or grit your teeth! On the plus side, farmers do not seem to experience the worst effects of "man 'flu" that other men seem to get, they just get on with the work without too much complaint.

Farmers wives are single mums

Children tend to partake in lots of activities once they get to about six years of age. The times for driving kids to and fro coincides with the evening milking. If you are married to a part-time farmer who works full-time off farm, his time for doing his farm work is in the evenings. Being married to a farmer means that you are probably living a reasonable distance (20-30 minutes drive) from activities. This means you are the sole taxi service and you have to wait for the hour or two until the activity is over, as it is not worthwhile driving home and back again. I do my grocery shopping when the children are at Cubs.

Enjoying a lazy morning in bed tends to be rare in farming households. If he is up at six, you feel you have had a lie on when the children wake you at 7:30 on a weekend morning. You might have friends who go to the hairdresser on a Saturday morning while their nine-to-five husbands bring the children to football. Forget about the hairdresser – you will be standing at the side of the football ground. Fancy a quiet peaceful hour in the evenings? You might get it when waiting in the car outside a Scout hut. Badminton halls seem to be located in the middle of nowhere but the plus side is that you can sit at the side of a freezing court and watch, read a book or chat to other parents.

Scrubbing up well

Farmers are not necessarily known for their fashion sense. They tend to be strongly recognisable as farmers when out shopping or doing business in town. Most wear hard wearing jeans, t-shirts or polo shirts, warm jumpers, wellies or boots and yes, their jeans are well splattered with muck on occasion. Do not expect him to shave too often, especially during busy harvesting or calving times. Visits to the barber can be rare during busy times of the year too.

You may become so accustomed to seeing each other look scruffy that when both of you dress up for a night out, you realise what a handsome couple you make and why you got married in the first place. Falling in love all over again happens frequently when married to a farmer.

Shopping trips

Farmers do not tend to go shopping very often. It tends to be limited to visits to barber, the electrical supplier and the veterinary surgery. At Christmas time, they may multi-task a little more and pop into a jewellery shop after visiting the barber. It is very rare that he does a grocery shop. However, once you announce that you are going to town to do the grocery shopping, buy a new dress and get your hair cut, he suddenly comes up with his own shopping list as it starts to tick inside his brain. He says, "Can you go to the veterinary lab with a sample? (this means you have a jar of cattle pooh in a plastic bag on the floor of your car)." Can you call to Pet and Vet? Can you collect a power drill? Can you leave the chainsaw in to be repaired?"

Once every two or three years, he accompanies you to a shopping centre. He needs a new suit for a wedding and plans to purchase jeans and shirts too. He is always amazed by the crowds and the prices. He starts complaining about tired feet within an hour, partly because he is unaccustomed to wearing shoes and partly because manoeuvring amongst the crowds means he has to take small steps – he much prefers long strides across the fields. Choose a nice boutique with seating and magazines for the men and you may get some peace – and his opinion on your own purchases.

What happens when you offer to help

It is a beautiful late summer's evening, you fancy a walk and as you know the cows need to be collected, it seems a good idea to multi-task and enjoys an evening stroll while bringing in the cows to be milked. You know it will take about 20 minutes. The farmer has been delayed so you give him a ring and offer to bring in the cows. You hear hesitancy as he considers whether to wait until he comes home and do it himself or list off all the jobs that need to be done en route to the cows.

It ends up taking you an hour. You have to open and close wires, herd the heifers en route, check a water trough and close a gate. As the cows are reluctant to leave the field and only walk when you are right beside them, it takes ages to round them up as the dog is with the farmer. You get into the cows' languid way of moving, you have time to pick a few wild flowers or a few blackberries. You can daydream and just let thoughts roam through your calmed mind. You enjoy the feeling of the sun on your back and the breeze on your face, and yes, even the squelch of mud under your

boots. It may end up taking you three times the length of time you thought it would, but time out in a busy day is time well spent. You were relaxing as well as working – what could be better?

His preoccupation with the weather

Farmers are constantly fascinated by the weather forecast. If one forecast is not delivering the news he wants, he checks another one online or phones a weather line. If he is listening to one on the phone, everyone has to be completely silent or risk his wrath.

The weather can do "what it says on the tin" during the winter months. We expect it to be cold and wet and it usually obliges, occasionally with too much frost and snow but it is not unexpected. Sunny days are a treat and if you get a stretch of them in February and early March and manage to get the cows and young lambs out to grass early, it is a huge bonus. In the spring and summer, the weather is crucial and can make or break your financial year. The work can become all-consuming if it isn't going to plan. You become accustomed to constantly seeing the weather forecast on TV, listening to it on the radio, phoning the weather line and checking it online, trying to determine which one is likely to be accurate and whether the vague "isolated showers" report means that rain will fall in your area.

The beauty of rain

Ireland is known as the Emerald Isle for the various shades of green in its landscape. Our mild, damp climate makes sweet grass, the most natural of foods for our livestock. Even though it is reasonably certain that rain falls every single week of the year, the Irish still tend to be very preoccupied with the weather and when it will rain next. Although we might find constant rain depressing, there is an exhilarating feel to soft rain with a little wind as you stride through the fields. Even harsh driving rain can lift the spirits if you are dressed for the weather.

It is rumoured that the Inuit have forty different words for snow. The Irish may not boast forty terms for rain but we come close.

20 Irish terms for rain

Types of rain	What they Mean
Soft rain	Rain that falls softly on your skin and on the grass.
Mist	Soft rain that you can barely see or feel, it is almost like wet air.
Drizzle	Soft rain that soaks you in minutes even though it might seem like a heavy mist.
A grand soft day	Soft rain on a warm day, perfect for growth.
April showers	Short bursts of heavy rain.
Cloudburst	A sudden heavy shower that does not last long.
A squib	An attempt at a shower.
Trying to rain	The clouds are heavy, the air feels heavy as though a thunderstorm is due.
Driving rain	Rain that lashes against your window and your windscreen, harsh and relentless.
Lashing rain	Heavy rain, falls in straighter lines than 'driving rain'.
Sun showers	Sunny days with sudden showers that disappear as quickly as they arrive.

Torrential rain	Heavy relentless and constant rain.
Heavens opened	A sudden and heavy shower of rain.
Spitting rain	Large drops of angry rain which soak you the moment you step outside. It almost hurts your skin as it feels spiky.
Pouring rain	Relentless heavy rain (similar to torrential rain).
A downpour	A sudden, long and very heavy shower of rain.
Pelting rain	A heavy version of spitting rain.
Thunder shower	A sudden heavy shower of rain during hot weather.
Shocking rain	Rain that is so heavy, the water just runs off the land.
Raining cats and dogs	I think we borrowed this from the English but it means very heavy rain – rain that is so heavy you wouldn't be surprised to see other objects appear amongst the drops.

Weather forecasters seen to be deliberately vague and unless Ireland is in the middle of a very unlikely dry spell, rain will feature somewhere in the forecast. Most of their predictions mean it will rain somewhere in the country.

Mainly dry	It will rain somewhere.
Occasional showers	It will rain somewhere.
Rain and drizzle	We can't tell you the extent of the rain.
Well scattered showers	It will rain somewhere.
Misty in the afternoon	Some rain.
Rain at times	It will rain somewhere.

It is not just farmers who talk about the weather constantly. Perhaps it is a nod back to our largely agricultural past when a much bigger proportion of the population were involved in agriculture. Perhaps it is because it is always changing, we often have four seasons in one day. While others might be concerned about having to water their gardens or enjoy a day at the seaside, the weather has a huge impact on farming practices, finances and success.

I am not sure whether I am disorganised or an eternal optimist but I never carry an umbrella. Given the prevalence of rain here, I am sure it is just carelessness but I like to think of it as cheerfulness. After all, there are worse things than getting wet!

Home produce

As far as the farmer is concerned, there is nothing healthier than his own creamy milk, cooled and straight from the bulk tank. Do not even suggest buying milk. You might as well dilute it with water as far as he is concerned, and as for skimmed milk, it is considered to be pure water!

If you have always liked the idea of setting up your own business and you have a flair for baking and food science, starting to produce your own creations from your kitchen table is perfectly possible on a farm. If you take time off work when the children are small, it is great to be able to start a part-time business that works around your lifestyle. What could be better than using produce from the farm and adding value to it? You can test it on consumers, starting small and selling it at country or farmers markets. Whether you are baking your own cupcakes, making jams and cheese or bottling apple juice, a farm provides an opportunity to create a family business.[60]

Many successful businesses started from the farmhouse kitchen table. Everyone knows that Irish produce ranks amongst the best in the world. From little acorns do mighty oaks grow – just look at food producers such as Glenilen, Gee's Gourmet Jams and Glenisk as your inspiration.

Sustainable farming

I would imagine that vegetarian farmers are few and far between. Many farmers eat their own produce with gusto. Apart from the daily provision of eggs from hens and ducks, milk from the cows or goats and the vegetables from the garden, you can have your freezer filled with a beef heifer, lamb, pig or even a goat. The good news is that the butcher does most of the work for you in preparing the bigger animals for the freezer. If you have chickens or ducks, you will both have the fun of wringing necks, plucking and cleaning out. Each mouthful will be savoured and enjoyed as long as you didn't give them "human" names. Eating a "Henry" or "Matilda" is just not the same as eating a pig called "Rashers".

The farming gait

Most people know a farmer instantly – there is something about those long strides, the rolling walk and the arms held out to the side like he is permanently carrying two full buckets. If they are in any doubt, a glance at gnarled and

welted hands will confirm his farmer status. You can play a game of "spot the farmer" when out shopping or on holidays.

You find yourself wondering if you are now identified by your own version of the farming walk. Are you holding those two shopping bags, albeit full of clothes from a boutique on a rare shopping trip, as though they are two buckets of milk for the calves?

Emergency teas

Forget the five barley loaves and two small fish. It inevitably happens that when there is hardly anything to eat in the house, you are expected to perform a minor miracle. There may be half a pan loaf, two eggs, a lump of cheese and half a tub of natural yoghurt left in the fridge and you get a text to say two contractors have arrived and will be in for tea in an hour. The shops are closed and in any case, you have neither the time nor the enthusiasm to drive to town. You find yourself becoming adept at creating a wonderful meal out of five ingredients.

Signature dishes

There is bound to be some dish or meal, be it brown bread, scones, a dessert or a Sunday roast that your mother-in-law makes and that you will never ever be able to emulate. Never even try. I repeat NEVER EVEN TRY. If you do happen to make it just as nice or nicer, your husband will be trapped between the two of you, your MIL will never forgive you for supplanting her efforts and you will have to make it regularly. Instead, let her bring it with her each time she visits or she can cook it for her son whenever you are away and they will both enjoy it.

Creating your own signature dish comes highly recommended. Not only is it be handy to know what you are baking when you are going to community, school or parish events, but if it is a firm favourite, people will look forward to it. My own signature dish is a chocolate biscuit cake, popular with adults and children. It is so popular and very easy to make so my recipe is as closely protected as a state secret. Never reveal your secrets if your recipes are hugely popular.

Farmhouse entertaining

Do you remember a time when you sat up until 3am over bottles of wine, putting the world to rights over a scrumptious dinner with friends, finished off with coffee and brandies? Long dinner parties for friends with good wine and stimulating conversation become a thing of the past when you marry a farmer. That is, unless you are a domestic goddess and are capable of cleaning the house, decorating the table, cooking dinner and getting children to bed before your husband arrives in from farming and your guests ring the doorbell. Getting up with the lark means that late dinner parties may be few and far between on the majority of farms. Large dinner parties are relegated to feeding the silage contractors their dinner and tea.

If you get together with other farmers for a meal or a beer after the haymaking, the conversation is not about world politics or the latest film or book. Instead, the conversation is punctuated with comparisons of grass growth, of lamb and beef prices, of fertilizer and feed prices and silage quality. You discuss the merits of topping, the price of meal, protein percentage in milk, AI sires, submission rates and other essential topics. Once you can chat about these topics with the best of them, you know you have really settled into farming life!

Cooking for contractors

It is highly likely, that as a farmer's wife, you have to feed the silage or harvest contractors. This seems to depend on the part of the country you are in. Some bring their own food and won't darken your door. Others are horrified if they are not being fed. It is a long working day and they do need nutritious meals to keep them going during the harvest season, whether provided by themselves or the farmer's wife.

There are two ways to go about this – you either slave all day over a hot stove, cooking a roast, carving it, making a fruit crumble for dessert, baking brown bread, scones and cakes, cooking a fry for tea, making five sliced pans of sandwiches and huge flasks of tea and bringing them to the field. You will be passing out from the heat of the oven and panicking over the roast drying up or getting cold if they are late. You may have inherited one of those 1980s hostess trolleys loved by all MILs, which keep dinners hot without drying out.

I like making life easier for myself, especially where cooking is concerned. You can simplify things by making the cooking of meals as easy as possible. Cooking huge casseroles makes life easier as everything is in one pot and if the men are half an hour late, it is not going to matter. If they are two hours late it will be a tad unpalatable but by then they are so hungry, they scarcely notice (or so I tell myself). Strawberries from the garden or a frozen strudel make yummy desserts. Always have icecream in the freezer. You might find some of them have horrified expressions at the prospect of fresh fruit, so icecream makes a handy and much-appreciated alternative. Although you will have to make sandwiches if they need food in the field, let them make their own sandwiches if they are eating supper at the table. Just put the bread and salad in the middle of the table and they can help themselves. In terms of baking cakes, I find making a biscuit cake in advance is handy (it defrosts quickly from the freezer too) and is ideal when you are not sure whether they will actually be coming or not.

Contractors never seem to think of their tummies until they have actually arrived in the field or they get hungry. They have no concept that it may be difficult to cook a dinner for eight men with little warning, when the meat is still in the freezer and you live ten miles from the nearest butcher.

One particularly inclement summer, the silage men kept promising they would come to cut but they never arrived. When they eventually drove into the yard, the promised rain had started an hour before. I was not a happy farmerette, not just because I had already shopped for them but because the grass quality was going to deteriorate if it rained for the next few days as it was forecast to do. It was five days before the silage was dried out to some extent so they could cut. I was not ready to forgive even though they were giving up their Sunday to cut our silage.

Contractors tend to be quite fussy about their food; they like plain meat (chicken, beef, or bacon) and potatoes, and the vegetables shouldn't be any more exotic than carrots or peas. Two weeks before, when I was serving up dinner for two contractors who had arrived unexpectedly, I asked if they were okay with the vegetable lasagne.

"Oh, yes, we'll eat anything," came the reply.

"Will you eat goat?" I asked thinking of what was in the freezer and what I would give them the following day.

"Goat! Goodness, no, we wouldn't eat goat!"

What was I going to give these silage men for their Sunday roast? Going to the freezer (I had refused to prepare anything until they were actually in the yard); I was just about to pull out some chicken fillets when I spied the goat chops. We love the little goat chops but are not so keen on the larger gigot chops. We had killed two goats earlier in the year and eaten lots of little chops and three goat legs. I started pulling out the gigot chops. I had about 24, so there was plenty for eight men.

In they trooped for their dinner, and as usual, they came in gradually, so some were almost finished their main course as I was serving it up for others. Now that I knew I didn't have any "extra men", I could offer them an extra goat chop. I could tell they weren't quite sure what they were eating. They had a fair idea it wasn't lamb, and some of the chops were a little overdone too. I could see one young lad look at another guy as if to say "What on earth is this?".

"Would you like some more goat?" I asked sweetly.

One man who had finished eating blanched "Is that what it is?" he asked.

"Yes", I replied "And when you're driving out again, you'll see next year's dinner in the field".

It was a quiet meal.

Goat meat is lovely; it is becoming increasingly popular here in Ireland, and rightly so. In one way, perhaps I wasted it on them as they didn't appreciate it. However, if a farmerette cannot have a giggle at others' expense every now and then, it would be a sad world.

"Extra men" refers to young lads who travel on the tractors with the contractors. Sometimes it is a younger brother or a nephew, occasionally it is a neighbour. One summer, eight contractors were sitting at the table and in walked a teenager with my father (who had seen him sitting on the tractor and invited him in for dinner). They sat down in the two remaining places at the extended table and I served up more casserole and didn't think any more about it, although I wondered why none of the men were talking to him. I discovered later that he was a young lad who had come over to them on the outfarm and asked them for a ride on the tractor for a while. To this day, I have no idea who he was.

Good time for babies

The timing of the birth of babies can be tricky; conception and birth seem to happen to suit themselves rather than your diary. However, there are certain times of the year when it is not a good idea to have a baby. That is, if you want your husband to be at the birth and to be there to change a few nappies, bond with the baby, and bring the baby to you for a feed. If you have a baby during the lambing or a busy harvest, you will be left to your own devices. On the other hand, having a baby during a busy calving or lambing time might have its advantages – you are both up half the night, and it should not be too difficult to feed a baby at the same time as keeping an eye on the calving monitor. He can always change a nappy while he is up checking on pregnant cows too.

Do not plan on conceiving during the lambing/calving time – if your husband is getting a maximum of two hours' sleep on average for a fortnight, sex is going to be the last thing on his mind, as are shaving and changing his socks!

Paperwork

As with all businesses, paperwork is crucial. For the farmer who works long hours on his own, keeping up to date with paperwork can be a constant battle. It is more than keeping a record of sales and purchases. All medicinal records, sires and dams, records for sprays and all the registering of new births (and any deaths) have to be recorded.

I hate paperwork with a vengeance. When I worked in an office in my early twenties, I was relatively organised and even achieved strange feelings of satisfaction when I had completed a batch of filing. I am not sure what happened during my metamorphosis over the years but the mathematical part of my brain definitely shrank and I developed apathy towards anything to do with filing or paperwork.

When I was a child, the passports for each animal (otherwise known as blue cards) were stored in a specific drawer in the utility. However, it frequently happened that the one card that was needed at any one time would be the card that was missing from the drawer and the house would have to be turned upside down until it was found. The missing card was often found in the tractor where my father had left it for some obscure reason.

After twenty years of marriage, my husband eventually recognised that taking over the paperwork was going to be cheaper than a divorce. He inputs much of the data on his smart phone in any case. It has been heaven since, there has been no more (or very little) of "Where's that piece of paper; I left it on the table two days ago; I said it had to go into the file; I saw it on the dresser; where did you put it...." At least an hour would be spent looking the crucial piece of paper. It has happened occasionally that I have rung a company and said that an important piece of paper did not arrive in the post, only to find it two days later. We now have a file that is so organised and so tidy that part of me wants to stroke it in awe and admiration.

Paperwork is crucial, so before you get close to divorce over it, decide:

- Which of you has the most natural ability to be organised?
- Which of you has more time – realistically?
- Whether to share it. If he does the medicines, you do the invoices.
- If neither of you can manage it, do get a book-keeper. It will work out cheaper than a divorce.

Farming for children

Farming provides children with a wonderful childhood. Yes, there are dangers and steps have to be taken to secure children in the garden and playing area so they do not arrive unaccompanied in the farmyard. Kids love "helping" by travelling on the tractor, bringing home straw or spreading fertiliser. Bringing in the cows or herding tends to be a favourite too. They also learn how to amuse themselves with the simplest of things. While you are drenching lambs in the pouring rain or giving cattle their copper boluses, the children will be jumping from bale to bale in the hay barn or learning how to measure out medication.

Farming is a great way to encourage kids to be entrepreneurial. They become part of the labour force on a farm quite early, whether they are putting all the passports in numerical order, bringing in the cows or standing in gaps, there is always work to be done on a farm. They can earn their own money by baking, helping out with tasks, selling hens' eggs or vegetables with an honesty box at the gate. As they get older, buying and selling their own piglets, lambs or calves offers them plenty of scope to try and make money.

Children learn about death in a matter of fact way. While they will be upset if a pet lamb or pet goat kid dies, a mock funeral seems to put their mind at ease. We once lost a pet goat kid called Herbie and the children were devastated. We dug a hole on the hill, put him in a box, covered it with earth and stones and laid a cross, and we all said a little prayer. It was amazing how quickly they recovered after they said goodbye. Children become accustomed to death on the farm and seem to accept it happens to animals and to people.

Our son was about five years old when a calf died and I was walking up the yard with our daughter and explaining that the sick calf had gone to heaven.

"No, he hasn't," said my son as he ran out of the hay barn, "He's still in the shed."

Picnics become overrated – going for a picnic is no longer seen as a treat but a relatively everyday occurrence of dinner in the field. There always seems to be some pandemonium beforehand as the boxes are packed with all the necessary crockery, condiments and cutlery. Hot tea is milked and sugared in the flasks. The children and the boxes go into the car before the hot casserole dish is wrapped in tea towels and put on the floor of the car. Saying to the children that you are going on a farm picnic may be greeted with groans, while their city cousins jump up and down with excitement.

Orienteering

Finding your way around the farm can be trickier than it sounds. Very few farms in Ireland are laid out as neat rectangular paddocks with car roads running between them. The reality tends to be haphazard jigsaw shapes separated by dense hedging and dykes. Each field has a name – some are named after tenant farmers that are long gone. Others will refer to something in it or from its past e.g. The Banks refers to the open cast mines that were once in it, the Quarry Field refers to the quarry or sandpit contained within it, The Letter Box once had a letter box on the other side of its hedge, the Big Field is the largest field on the farm at 27 acres. Some will be less obvious – the Top bottom field, the One off the Quarry Field, the Top of the Lawn or the Middle Field.

Why do you need to know the names of the fields? Sooner or later you will get a phone call asking you to bring a tractor part or his dinner to him in the field. He will be in a hurry, so if you need directions, they will be barked at you and you will be left feeling totally confused. Surprising him with a picnic in the field on a sunny day is a nice idea too but it is not always a good idea to surprise him. Accidents can happen. You drive across the field thinking he is waving hello to you, whereas he was actually trying to warn you about the huge hidden dyke in the middle of the field. You leave the gate to the field open when you drive in and some cattle escape while you are eating your tasty lunch. Or he may not realise that you are driving close by and opens the sprayer on the slurry spreader.

Fitness

Living in the countryside means you can get your exercise with brisk walks down sweet smelling honeysuckle filled hedges – if you want to take your life into your own hands. The problem with narrow country roads is that car drivers fly along them as though they don't expect to meet another car. They certainly don't expect a pedestrian, who has to jump quickly into the overgrown ditch with its stinging nettles and deep dyke.

The good news is that you save on gym fees, as you will be getting exercise from chasing cattle, feeding calves and throwing tyres on top of the silos. Covering the silage pit is certainly one job that demands a degree of strength, patience and fitness. Silage (cut grass) is preserved by packing it tightly into a huge pit and covering it with two layers of black polythene which are then kept in place by tyres (if it is an outdoor pit) or dried dung (if it is indoors).

Sound easy? Hmmmm, try standing on top of a silage pit on a breezy day when every gust of wind lifts the polythene. It is your job to keep an eye on the children and keep the polythene in place while the farmer brings the anchoring heavy tyres or the first load of dung. Children have to sit or lie in position with instructions not to move while you keep an eye on them. Once the polythene is secure, there is the job of flinging the tyres into position. Do you remember throwing the discus in school? It is very similar. You grab the rim of a tyre with your strongest arm, balance it against your hip for a second, pull back your arm about eighteen inches to get a good swing and hurl it as close to the desired position as you can. If it is not hurled fast enough, the dirty rainwater that has gathered inside will splash out all over you, so that is a very good reason for increasing your throwing power.

Management of your time

One of the beauties of being self employed is you can decide on your own timetable – to an extent. Murphy's Law tends to have a hand in it though. Just when you think you have the day planned, something will go wrong. A piece of machinery will break down and you will receive a phone call that goes something like this:

"Are you planning on going to town today'?

"No, why"?

"A part has gone on the mower, I rang xxxx, and they'll have a spare part there at two o'clock".

"Ok, I'll drive in for it later then".

"Well, if you're sure; if not, I'll go".

Sigh.

"No, it's okay, I hadn't much planned for today anyway, and I might as well do a grocery shop while I'm in too".

"Can you call to Pet & Vet too? I need some dry cow tubes".

Suddenly the peaceful afternoon has turned into a three hour shopping trip.

When he rings to find out what time dinner will be and you tell him ten minutes, woe betide you if he comes in after ten minutes and it isn't ready. Farmers seem to expect that the dinner will be on the table for them at the exact minute they walk in the door. It doesn't matter how many times I explain that if I did put it on the table at the allotted dinner time, it would usually be stone cold by the time he made it in. That information just doesn't register. They often tell you they will be half an hour and arrive in two hours later.

Holidays

You are self employed, so you can go on holidays whenever you like – as long as the livestock are sorted and it isn't the harvest, calving or AI season. The bank balance has to be agreeable too. Farmer husbands often tend to be reluctant to go on holidays – part of it can also be due to the work and hassle involved in ensuring everything is left in tip top shape for the relief workers, part of it can be due to the fact that he knows he will miss the farm. If he is a dairy farmer, expect him to look a little morose at milking time as he wonders how his cows are getting on without him. If you have managed to tear him away for a week, he will be getting into the holiday mood by day three. However, a day or two before you head home; you will notice a change again. Instead of being miserable at milking time, he will start to look cheerful as he looks forward to seeing his lovely ladies.

If he decides to stay at home while you go somewhere with the children for a few days, you have three choices. If your mother-in-law is nearby, it can be a good idea to let her have her son back and "feed him up a bit" with his old favourites. If she's not nearby, then you might leave pre-cooked meals in the freezer. There is no point buying frozen ready meals as they "wouldn't feed a sparrow". Remember, he needs his meat, spuds and two vegetables. The other alternative is to buy a few packs of rashers and some loaves of bread and let him live on bacon, bread and butter for the week. Bake a huge fruit cake and he will slather each slice with a wedge of butter. He will enjoy slumming it and will appreciate freshly cooked meals when you get home.

Housekeeping

One of the things about living in a farmhouse is that it really is a home. If you are after a showhouse that is pristine and tidy, living on a farm is unlikely to make that possible. You will find all kinds of unexpected small farming paraphernalia and accessories in your farmhouse when you are married to a farmer. Stray bits of calf meal that catch in a trouser crease roll out onto the bathroom floor; you will find containers of colostrum in your freezer and various receipts on the bedside table. The end of the kitchen table becomes home to numerous copies of farming newspapers, AI catalogues, invoices and breeding charts. It encroaches on your eating area until you take the bull by the horns and decide to tidy it up, knowing that in two hours' time he will be looking for one precious piece of paper you just moved.

Did you picture a beautiful farmhouse kitchen complete with an Aga perfect for baking homemade bread, and creating a cosy reading nook beside it? That Aga becomes home to various tiny pet lambs during the lambing season, as they are restored to life by its steady warmth. Wet coats and hats are draped around it and a lovely farming aroma wafts around the kitchen! If the farmer is in the kitchen, it is impossible to walk out of the back door without falling over his dirty wellies and the adoring cattle dog.

Overdraft

The words "farming" and "overdraft" go together like "Bonnie and Clyde". An overdraft becomes your best friend, albeit reluctantly, as you wonder if the farm bank account will ever be in the black again. The milk cheque goes in and the payments for loans, fertiliser and feed go out, as well as your wages to your personal account. The Single Farm Payment comes in but the "tax man" has to be paid. Sometimes too much money goes out before the milk cheque goes in and this is flagged by the bank.

The intelligence of man's best friend

Good cattle and sheep dogs are worth their weight in gold, particularly when they can equal a couple of men in their rounding up abilities. They are good company too; a farmer is never alone when he can chat to a dog. Dogs respond to shouts and whistles, they usually do their utmost to please and they respond well to a quick rub down. A simple "that'll do now" tells them the job is finished.

When a dog remembers what the farmer is supposed to do next and he has forgotten, you start to wonder who should be running the show. My farmer had been feeding meal to the cattle using the large bucket on the loader. For the next job, which involved feeding a bale to the cattle across the lane, he needed to change the bucket for the bale fork. Driving up, he wondered where the dog was, as he usually jumped into the loader with him. He was annoyed, because the dog keeps the bulls in the shed while he pushes in the bale. He reached the yard and discovered he had forgotten to remove the loader bucket and put on the bale fork. Cursing again and returning to the farm yard, he wondered where the sheepdog was. He was sitting patiently beside the bale fork, waiting for his master to come with the loader to put it on. Such a smart dog.

To see a good dog work hard, partly because he enjoys it, partly to get praise and please his owner and partly because he is so intelligent, is a joy to behold. A good dog works like poetry in motion.

More farmerish than the farmers themselves

Being married to a farmer takes adjustment, especially if you are from a town. However, many "townie" wives have become better and more dedicated farmers than the farmers themselves, so don't be afraid of getting stuck in. The trick now is to stay married and celebrate that diamond anniversary in years to come.

Section 5

How to Stay Married

Your husband is standing in the cattle crush at the rear end of a cow. When he shouts for help, and then adds "you'll need gloves", you know it is not going to be pretty or sweet-smelling!!

Being A Farmwife

Being married to a farmer provides many opportunities that create fun and adventure, as well as hard work. If he is a full-time farmer, there are usually three scenarios for the farming partner. You may work full-time outside the home, you might work with him on the farm and share the child-minding, or you might set up your own business using products or facilities on the farm. Running businesses in tandem on the farm means lots of hard work, but as is true with many businesses, it is not the achievement that is the most fun but the journey towards the goals.

You will have learnt quite a few things about yourself since you first married the farmer:

1. You can multi-task pretty effectively.

2. You can swear with the best of them.

3. Your map-reading has improved substantially.

4. Your driving and spatial awareness is much better now.

5. You can hold a conversation with anyone about cows, sheep, goats, wind turbines or genetically modified crops.

6. You are much more relaxed – finding calf nuts rolling around on the bathroom or utility floor doesn't freak you out anymore.

7. You are much more confident and are quite happy to go to events on your own. This, of course, is because you were forced to do so as he was not able to make it at the last minute, yet again.

8. You think you should have been a nurse, a midwife or a vet after all.

9. You are much more relaxed about meal times – as long as the family eats a main meal at some stage during the day, it works.

10. You feel rich when the bank account is in credit.

11. You discovered there was a hugely optimistic person inside you bursting to get out for years. You can find a silver lining on every single cloud.

12. You find yourself flicking through the *Farmers Journal* in the evenings, whereas it used to be *Hello* magazine.

13. You can read your husband's mind from fifty paces, though not always when sorting cattle.

14. You wish you had a farmer's wife of your own – then you could really kick some ass and run this country by becoming the IFA President and then the Minister for Agriculture.

Farmer V 9-5

Being married to someone who works in a nine-to-five job in the city is not the same as being married to a farmer. There are distinctly different challenges and pressures, different family lives to that of friends and varied hours of work. Both systems of living have their own advantages and disadvantages – it is when you are married to a 9-5er who is also a part-time farmer that the fun really starts!

Working 9-5	Working as Farmers
Good holidays – maybe even 32 days holidays a year plus bank holidays.	Get away for a 32 hour summer break.
Plenty of free time in the evenings – although that does depend on the commute and if deadlines are looming.	Working late is often the norm. Finish at 6pm for two months during the winter.
Most weekends off.	Sunday afternoons off.
Alarm goes at 7:00am unless there is long commute.	Often up by 6am.
Share domestic duties.	A farmer has little time for cooking and house chores.
Do the grocery shopping together.	The farmer might go grocery shopping about once a year – perhaps when you are on holidays or ill.
Going away for weekends can happen spontaneously.	Even a few hours away takes careful planning, especially if a relief milker is needed.
Monday morning blues.	Every day of the week is the same so never have Monday morning blues
Happy Friday feelings.	Saturday is the favourite day – no salesmen calling, no post, no phone calls.
Occasionally away for business trips.	Never away.
Sleepless night due to stress and targets.	Always have a good night's sleep, unless it is during the calving season.

Can take special days off work to celebrate (deadlines and meetings permitting) e.g. birthdays, anniversaries.	Own boss. Only answers to the animals and the weather. Can take days off if they do not coincide with silage, drainage, reseeding, haymaking, straw loading...
If you aim to leave by 10 am, you'll be driving out the gate at 10:15 am.	If you aim to leave at 10 am, you'll be driving out the gate at 11:45 am.
Can switch off relatively easily when away from work.	If away on holidays, he will always think of the cows at milking time.
Dinner parties.	Cook for silage men!
Probably on time for dinner.	Could be one or two hours late for dinner.
You can spend any evening in the garden.	Gardening is relegated to occasional Saturday and Sunday afternoons.
Time off can be spent at home and it feels like time off.	For true time off, you have to get away from the house/farm for the day.
You share the driving when you travel together.	You usually drive. He sleeps or is entertained by looking to see what is happening over the hedges.
You share the parenting equally.	You are like a single parent for ten months of the year.
You both share bringing children to activities.	He brings them once a year.
You get to spend some Saturday mornings at the hairdressers.	You spend Saturday mornings feeding calves, moving cattle or on the sideline of a football pitch.
He sees cutting the grass or putting out the bins as jobs for the man of the house.	You do it – it is connected to the house so it is seen as your domain!!

Decorating or DIY can be done all year round.	He can only do it during the two "dry" months of the year (dairy farmer) so you save it for him for all those early evenings when he is in at 6pm.
Smart shirts and suits need ironing.	Farming clothes require a roll or a fold.
Commuting time to work can be significant.	Commute is measured in seconds – from kitchen to yard.
He isn't available for childcare during the day.	He can be somewhat flexible to look after children after school if needed.

Advantages of being a farmer's wife

There are many advantages to being a farmer's wife. Sometimes they can seem a bit dubious but when you consider everything you enjoy, it is not a bad life at all.

1. You do not have to pay gym membership. You build up your arm and leg muscles feeding calves twice a day for a couple of months. You can walk, jog or run across beautiful green fields - as long as you wear wellies for nine months of the year.

2. If you are the type of person who likes your own space, you will love the seclusion of farm life and because your husband works all the hours under the sun, you need not worry about him being under your feet.

3. If you dream of writing or painting for a living or any other creative career, living in splendid isolation means that your creativity will be stimulated daily by the beautiful views and being closer to nature.

4. Being self employed, you choose when you work and when you have time off. This is perfect as long as you don't want time off every morning and evening!

5. Being rurally based, there are lots of community and parish events for which baking is a necessity. If you like cooking and baking, you will be in heaven with plenty of opportunities to try new recipes and perfect them for the county show competitions.

6. Do not worry introducing about yourself to anyone when you first move in - everyone knows exactly who you are. Your assets and heritage will have been discussed at length within a forty mile radius.

7. You can enjoy romantic picnics with your loved one - indeed, it is expected that you bring dinner to the field when he is busy working all day on the out farm.

8. Nothing is better than working with your partner on the land, achieving a harvest and seeing the cycle of life every year.

9. The meaning of a family farm really comes home when your children are out helping you. Children enjoy collecting eggs or carrying milk to the calves in their little sandcastle buckets. By the time they are teenagers, they are capable of doing a full day's work and can almost earn their own keep!

Pre and Post Nuptial Agreements

In the past, farming parents held onto the farm until they died, sometimes to retain control or because they needed an income. It is now happening again, partly due to the perceived risk of the younger couple splitting up and divorcing. "The spectre of an 'outsider' getting money or land in a court settlement is very real and is putting the fear of God into older farming families."[61]

Like all marriages, some farming marriages end in separation and divorce. Divorce is a relatively new phenomenon in Ireland, yet there are now 4,000 marriages ending every year and two out of every three divorces are filed by women. The decision to permit divorce was decided by a national referendum and many farmers and their wives were against divorce, believing it would destroy many family farms. One farmer's wife with nine children saw all potential farmers' wives as gold diggers, arguing that brides would be choosing older farmers. They would have a more established farm, so the brides would benefit more when it came to divorce.[62]

Irish farmers are passionate about their farms, so much so that land only exchanges hands once in every 400 years on average, with less than 0.5% of Irish land going on sale each year. Of that 0.5%, one in six farms are sold because of a marriage breakdown. This has repercussions on all the family members, from those who were emotionally attached to the land and handed it over, to the farmer whose ability to make a living from a smaller farm is now diminished, and to the children whose dreams of a farming livelihood may have been destroyed.

Land is a considerable asset, yet the income derived from it is often derisory in comparison to its value. Most farmers see themselves as custodians of the land, farming it for their lifetime, in preparation to hand over to the next generation. Selling part of their heritage, particularly if the farm has been in the same family for generations, is like selling part of the family. Many parents are delaying transferring the farm to their successor in case the marriage fails and half the farm is claimed by the daughter-in-law or son-in-law. Apart from not wanting to run the risk of losing part of the farm, some are thinking about their own financial security. There is a lesson here to all farmers – they need to be thinking about their retirement from a much earlier age.

Would you Marry a Farmer?

The delay of land mobility also has repercussions on the future of Irish farming as well as marriages. If sons are being treated as 'lads and labourers' they lose the ability to be progressive and forward-thinking. We run the risk of going back to the 1950s, with many farmers not inheriting until their parents had died. With 7% of farmers aged less than 35, 25% over 65 and the average age of farmers being 58 years, you can see that younger farmers are in the minority. The increased involvement of progressive and enthusiastic young farmers is crucial for agri-food progress. Young farmers cannot secure borrowing to improve the farm if the farm is not in their name. The delay of transfer hinders progress and improvement of individual farms, with ramifications for Irish farming in general. I would also imagine that living under the thumb of one's ageing parents is a pressure that could add significant angst to a young married relationship.

What seems worse is that many farmers are deliberately not getting married because they are afraid they are being wed for their farm. Some believe that a potential marriage partner might be a gold-digger, intending to take half their farm and leave them with very little. Perhaps it is better to have loved and lost than never loved at all, and look at pre-nuptial agreements as a safeguard if nothing else. After all, we are all custodians of our farms and if there is no heir, it will pass to another family in any case.

There have been calls for pre-nuptial agreements to be upheld should the marriage break down. At the moment, pre-nuptial agreements do not have a legislative or statutory basis in Irish law but judges are taking them into consideration. However, if a farm is not making sufficient income, the judge is less lenient toward the farmer. There have been renewed calls by the Irish Farmers Association to ensure that pre-nuptial agreements have a legal standing.[63] It has also been recognised at government level that the lack of legal clarity is affecting farm transfers significantly.[64]

How do the couples themselves feel about pre-nuptial agreements? Some farmers believe a marriage should be based on love and trust rather than a piece of paper declaring what each is entitled to should the marriage break down and that agreeing to one is a bad omen. Others feel it gives security against an unknown future and pre or post-nuptial agreements should form part of everyone's wealth planning. While not romantic, a pre-nuptial agreement should safeguard the safety and future of a family farm. It holds too that a successor wants the security of knowing he or she can pass the farm on to the next generation in a better condition than it was inherited.[65] Very few farming children see the farm as a gravy train, to be sold for monetary wealth.

Whether you have a pre-nuptial agreement for future finances or not, the fact remains that nobody wants their marriage to end in sadness or divorce. According to New Zealander Mark Townshend, farmers who have happy marriages have farms that thrive.[66] Therefore, the couple need to have a common goal for what they want to achieve for their family and that includes decisions regarding expansion and investment.

Perhaps the prenuptial agreement should also include the following:

- Romantic dates every so often.

- Sharing of vacuuming and cleaning the bathroom.

- Help with scrubbing the cooker, washing windows, cleaning the car.

- He could cook a dinner occasionally.

- Share the cheque books and bank accounts.

- Feeding contractors – or not.

- Milking cows – or not.

- Bringing dinners to the field – or not.

- Annual holiday together.

- One afternoon off most weeks of the year, even if it is only three hours off on a Sunday.

I wish I had negotiated on the one about feeding contractors!!

Irish farmers as husbands

According to an article in Irish Central, many women divorce their Irish husband because he is too much of a Mammy's boy.[67] He wants everything done for him, wants to be spoilt and refuses to help around the house. They also see Irish men as consuming too much alcohol and as being roving and lazy. Apparently, they tend to be chauvinist and refuse to go for counselling, because they see it as unmanly.

Some farmers are very domesticated, some aren't. Many have had their mammies looking after them all their lives and may think that meals appear miraculously on the tables, clean clothes arrive folded in their wardrobe and kitchen floors clean themselves. If your farmer is one of the latter, he needs a re-education.

Tips for a happy marriage

1. He needs to realise that clothes that are dropped on the bathroom or bedroom floor do not end up in the washing machine or the wardrobe on their own accord.

2. Pockets of jeans must be emptied before being put in the laundry basket or washing machine. Nuts, bolts, screws, cattle tags and other hard objects do not do a washing machine any favours. Hot soapy water does not do important folded receipts any favours either. Should any receipt be washed, it is bound to be the most important one that is required for a VAT refund.

3. Calf nuts and artificial fertiliser granules tend to accumulate and hide in the turn-ups and creases of jeans and roll into the most unlikely of places when jeans are removed. If you are building a new farmhouse, having a shower room close to the back door can be a good idea. If the work clothes are deposited there, it keeps that calf nut rolling to a minimum.

4. If the dirty clothes are in the laundry basket, you will presume that pockets have been emptied and it is safe to put them into the washing machine.

5. If you do decide to empty or check his pockets, do it with caution as all kinds of sharp implements are carried in a farmer's trouser pockets. Having your finger pierced by a fencepost staple's sharp edge is not to be recommended.

6. His mother may have ironed his farming clothes, but who is going to see him but the cows, the men at the creamery and an occasional agricultural salesman? Clean and folded (or rolled in a ball) clothes, what more should a man want?

7. Farmers' clothes tend to tear and rip, particularly jeans. They get caught on barbed wire or sharp edges of machinery. If you love sewing, that is great – you will have a job for life.

8. He should remember that farming clothes need to be washed on the hottest cycle.

9. Do not put a "good wash" or a "white wash" on straight after a "farming wash".

10. A farmer should realise that finding his socks under the bed is almost grounds to start divorce proceedings, particularly if it is calving time and he has been wearing them nonstop for the last three days.

11. When you have small children, there are days when a trip to the clothes line can feel like a major expedition. Being married to a farmer means he is always around and can multi-task by taking children herding with him or taking one to spread fertiliser.

12. When you have both been working hard all day, the farmer needs to realise that simple things such as filling the dishwasher, putting his own dirty clothes into the washing machine and knowing how to switch it on can make all the difference. Foreplay starts when he loads the dishwasher for you!

13. The farmer should be good at changing dirty nappies – after all, he is accustomed to spreading slurry and dung, and risks being sprayed with runny excreta twice daily in the milking parlour pit.

14. Multi-tasking is an essential skill for farm husbands and wives. Time management consultants may tell you that it is best to concentrate on one task at a time, that it is much more productive, but a cow will not wait for you to finish peeling the spuds while she is delivering a calf, nor will husband be happy about having to wait for his dinner because a cow was calving. If your husband is away at the mart, you have the task of keeping one eye on the television in the corner of the kitchen, the television that offers a blurry, black and white view of what is happening in the calving house. Nine times out of ten, the cow in question keeps her tail end firmly away from either of the two cameras so you have to keep running up to the maternity ward to check on her. I think my most efficient multi-tasking in this situation was when I managed to cook a dinner, check on a cow calving about five times (delivering a lovely heifer calf),

collect the children from the bus just before she delivered and answer a phone call – all in 40 minutes.

15. Money is the root of all evil and if there is a bad year in farming and money is tight, that is when pressures intensify and arguments can start. You might want a new kitchen and he might want a new calf shed or a new fertiliser spreader. Whichever offers a financial return is going to be the winner in terms of any debates, so there needs to be a regular salary coming from the farm each month which pays for living expenses, holidays and any non-essential work on the house and garden.

16. You know how frustrating and infuriating it is when essential household appliances such as the washing machine, boiler and dishwasher break down and need replacement in the same quarter. In farming, it happens that the dung spreader, the mower and the fertiliser spreader all need replacing in the one year. You may have plans for a holiday or a new kitchen and have to wave goodbye to them.

17. Apparently most male farmers don't tend to tell their partners they love them; they tend to say things like "I haven't said I don't, have I?" or "I'm still here, aren't I?"[68] Just ask him if he would prefer to sleep with his wife or his prize sheep after a tough financial year and he might appreciate you. Having said that, telling him that you and the children would like to see more of him will only earn you a retort that you can all go out and farm more!

18. Sometimes when we enjoy our work so much, we forget to indulge in some downtime and work seven days a week, even if it does not feel like work. Getting away from it all, even if it is just a Sunday afternoon each week, means that your batteries are recharged and you are giving yourself space to think outside the box.

19. Date nights can be rare in farming, particularly at busy times of the year. You need to be prepared to consider a tractor date as a date night, and he needs to be aware that planning a surprise night out during the quieter months will stand him in good stead for help during the busier months.

20. It would be rare to marry into a farming family with no family feuds in its history. There are so many things to feud about – inheritance, succession, land, dowries as well as all the things other families might argue about. Choose whether to try to make up or ignore them. Whatever you do, do not dwell on it. Life is short and it is there to be enjoyed.

21. If you can't beat them, join them. Even if you aren't into milking cows or driving big machinery, choose to do what you do enjoy. Cook and bake with fresh produce. Enter some competitions in local shows. Choose your own pet livestock. Discover how to make cheese, wine or butter. Start blogging. Enter cross country races. Learn how to crochet. Join the ICA or IFA. The opportunities are endless – just grab one or two.

22. Make memories to laugh about. I will never forget the year we reared chickens. My darling husband had

finished off plucking and cleaning out one of the last chickens in early December. The next morning, I opened the door to the back hall and screamed as I saw a dead Santa Claus standing there. A murdered Santa Claus with his white hair standing on top of his head and his white scraggly beard around a wide open mouth. It took me a very long two seconds to realise it was a huge chicken hanging there having been mostly plucked – a chicken which still had feathers sticking out of its head and out of the bottom end.

Mistress of your own domain

Building (or renting in the meantime) is essential – even if it is a tiny house, it will be your own. For generations, married couples have lived in the same house as his parents or his mother, with three generations sharing the one dwelling. While two women can share a house peacefully, this is a rare occurrence. The expense of building a separate house or "granny flat" might seem unwarranted at first, particularly if the mother-in-law is widowed and may need assistance or is lonely, yet it seems sensible to section off part of the house at the very least. When you consider your MIL has been mistress of the house for decades and you will want to put your own stamp on it, it is clear that two unrelated women are going to find it hard to adjust and live in harmony in a house together.

There are so many little things that can add up and lead to friction – who left the milk out, who was talking on the telephone for so long, and who didn't put away the hoover? Not to mention when it comes to decorating decisions – the MIL might love her terracotta hallway but you want to wallpaper it and hang new curtains, replacing her twenty year old net curtains. She might prefer to keep the toaster in a cupboard, you prefer it left out on the worktop. She prefers Lyons tea leaves, you prefer Barry's teabags ..... all the little things add up to cause irritation. With the arrival of children, it can only get worse. It can be hard enough sometimes for two parents to decide on parenting techniques, without a third party exercising a type of discipline you might not agree with. Three is a crowd and it will usually lead to fireworks, or one person wanting to bury the other under the patio. As stated in *Letters of a Matchmaker*, "If you were to build a house from here to Australia it wouldn't be big enough for two women. Where you have two women under the same roof, the marriage is under fire from the start. Two can make a nest but three can make hell".[69]

In rural Australia, one of the unwritten rules is to ensure that you cannot see your MIL's clothes line and she can't see yours. The last thing you want are comments on how your clothes have been hanging out for days, or how early or late your bedroom curtains were drawn and pulled.

Infertility & Succession

There are couples who choose to remain childfree, but the majority of couples reach a stage when they would like to have children. The stress and heartbreak of infertility is tough on every couple but it must be even more difficult for farming couples. You are surrounded by conception and births on the farm, with ewes going to the ram, cows being AI'd, animals being born and the constant reminder that barren animals are sent to the factory. It can seem that the whole world is getting pregnant and giving birth, from the latest 45 year old pregnant celebrity to the cows and the farm cats.

A lot of sex happens on the farm and much of it is in public – it can feel like you can't get away from it. The artificial insemination technician comes once or twice a day for a few months to inseminate the cows. The cows and heifers are monitored daily for signs of being on heat. The bull's fertility is checked before he is let out with the cows or heifers. The rams tup away with the ewes, the boar has his wicked way with the sows and as for the horses, we won't go there. Even the cockerel prances around.

There is a lot of trying to prevent conception too, mostly with the dogs. Many farmers believe that spaying or castrating a dog will make them fat and lazy and that they will not work as efficiently as before. The problem then is that a female dog will attract all the dogs in the vicinity, who will bark and howl as you drag her into the house and keep her there. Your male dog will go walkabout if he as much as sniffs a bitch on heat.

With an emphasis on succession in most farming families and neighbourhoods, many farmers find it difficult when there is no obvious successor to their farm. All farmers would like a child to carry on with another generation of farming. Being childless on a farm makes the issue of succession even tougher. Some farmers also find it difficult when children do not want to carry on with the farming tradition. It is one thing to decide that you can sell the farm at 65 and enjoy a glorious retirement but the reality is most farmers stay farmers until they are six feet under and many remain in farming until they just cannot farm anymore.

Only 12.4% of Irish farms are in female ownership, with most parents giving the farm to the eldest son. While some parents may be in the situation where they purchase a farm for a second son or decide which son is best suited to farming, there are not many farming parents who will consider a daughter for inheriting the farm if they have a son. Keeping the farm in the family name is also important to 23% of farmers.[70]

Women are to the forefront in organic farming and in smallholder farms. Some farmers might argue that tillage or dairy farming is not suitable for women. However, with the onset of machinery and labour saving devices, farming is not necessarily about physical strength any more, or it is certainly only a small portion of it. More and more women are going into veterinary science and I am sure it will only take a generation or so before the same happens in farming. Yes, there are some difficulties; for example, a pregnant woman should not work with lambing ewes as some infections can be transmitted during labour can cause miscarriage in humans.[71]

More parents are now discussing succession with all their children and decisions are made on suitability rather than gender. Succession facilitators are on hand to prevent decisions causing feuds and to ensure everyone is satisfied. Those who inherit are not necessarily going straight home to farm after school (as has been the case for generations) but are travelling and working abroad for a while – learning different farming practices and finding out what it is like to work for someone else. It will be interesting to see if the number of women farmers increases, women who are acknowledged as farmers in their own right.

Anniversary Gifts

If you get past the division of labour, spare money being spent on "farm essentials", coping with the darkness and the muck, surviving the "goldfish bowl" and learning how to drive big machinery, there will be plenty of anniversaries to celebrate. Did you remember to get married during a traditionally quiet month in farming terms? That will maximise the chances of a night out or a weekend away – you don't want him to have those readymade excuses. Farmers are not necessarily known for their romantic gestures and will use the excuse of being busy for not getting to town to buy birthday and anniversary presents.

You may pour your heart and soul into preparing a creative gift that will mean much to both of you. However, it is unlikely he will put the same preparation into surprise birthday or anniversary gifts. Unless he happens to be going to the mart and it is not too far from a jewellery shop, it is doubtful he will manage to get to town, buy a gift and get home again without you noticing.

On a positive note, because he rarely makes it to the jewellery or flower shop, they always mean so much more. Plus, a sporadic gift means it is an even bigger surprise.

Anniversary gifts might include:

- Artificial roses with artificial raindrops on them – because the florist told him they would last longer.
- Flowers from the garden – that is why you need to have a rose garden!
- Jewellery.
- Antique furniture.

- A new household gadget – you may get to the stage when you will actually be grateful for a decent vacuum cleaner.
- Perfume.
- A weekend away.

A good tip is to make friends with one of the people working in a jewellery shop and ensure he goes to her for assistance when picking out a gift. You nip in two weeks beforehand and show her the exact bracelet or necklace that you want. I remember a jewellery shop in Carlow being frequented by numerous farmers in the two days before Christmas. (It may still be the case) All of them went to the one salesperson who could be overheard saying things like "You got her the xxx necklace last year Jim. Why don't you get her the matching bracelet this year? Yes, we do have it in stock. Will I giftwrap it for you?" How perfect is that? You just have to drop hints and direct him towards particular shops and he will still believe he has surprised you.

If I were to do it all over again, would I marry a farmer?

We have been married for twenty-one years. Ten years were spent studying and working in 9-5 jobs, child-free, living in pretty Victorian terraced houses with weekends off and good holiday allowances. We returned to Ireland in 2002 and we have almost twelve years of dairy and beef farming under our belt. Yes, there have been challenges but that is life no matter what your occupation. Targets have to be met in most jobs just as much as they have to be reached in farming. We might have a bad year financially but I won't be fired! The cows and sheep rarely hold it against us if we are having a bad day and give them a bit of abuse. The cattle dog is the farmer's most admiring and loyal worker. Working together is fun as well as hard work.

Life is a journey and marriage is a journey together. We work together to meet challenges and create opportunities. We plan for the future with short term and long term goals. I'm the most impulsive one so the farmer has to rein me in sometimes. We may shout at each other when sorting cattle, we may bicker when we are tired but our love and respect for each other keeps growing. While I hanker after the walks in the New Forest and strolls around Salisbury occasionally, I would not swop being married to a farmer. Would you?

Don't forget to read more at www.irishfarmerette.com

You will find me on twitter at @IrishFarmerette and you can email me at Lorna@irishfarmerette.com

Would you Marry a Farmer?

Acknowledgements

There are so many people I would like to thank – without whom this book would still just be an idea or perhaps three unfinished chapters.

To my parents, Ruby and Joe, for entrusting us with Garrendenny Farm and for an idyllic rural childhood. To my brother Alden and his wife Eimear. To my sister Daphne and her husband Stewart and their three children, Zoe, Amy and Kyle.

I would like to thank all involved in the ACT Ireland Wales project, particularly James Moxey, Kieran Comerford and Terry O'Brien, as it was James's presentation on crowdfunding that convinced me take the bull by the horns and turn an idea into a reality.

To my illustrator Joanne Condon for interpreting my ideas so cleverly. To my editor Derbhile Graham for your expertise and help. To Amanda and Ian of Spiderworking for all your work with the website. It has been a pleasure to work with all of you – thank you.

The lines from 'The Great Hunger' by Patrick Kavanagh are reprinted from *Collected Poems*, edited by Antoinette Quinn (Allen Lane, 2004), by kind permission of the Trustees of the Estate of the late Katherine B. Kavanagh, through the Jonathan Williams Literary Agency.

"The Ballroom of Romance", from THE BALLROOM OF ROMANCE by William Trevor, copyright (c) 1965, 1966, 1969, 1971, 1972 by William Trevor. Used by permission of Viking Penguin, a division of Penguin (USA) LLC.

Thank you to everyone who supported me in the crowdfunding campaign – which includes FBD Insurance,

Tea Rooms at Ducketts Grove, Glenisk, Agriland.ie, Connolly's Red Mills, Wildways Adventures, Charisma Bootcamp, Pet Sitters Ireland, Farmers Sell Direct, Countrylife, Geraldine Lavin, Herbi and Carni, Farmers Forum, Pat Whelan, Bill King, Robert Jacob, Trish Reilly,

Tracy Jones, Bob Quinn, Tremayne Horkan, Carol Feighery, Francis Taaffe, Sue Corbett, Fionnuala Malone, Siobhan O'Beirne, Katy Walsh, Sian Phillips, Sorcha O'Neill, Hugh Leddy, Mona Wise, Margaret Flynn, Carol Tallon, Maura McDonnell, Brad Clements, Lily Collison, Naoimh Murphy, Jacqui McNabb, I couldn't have done it without you.

Twitter proved to be of immense support during the crowdfunding. To all of my twitter followers of @irishfarmerette, thank you.

To all those who filled out my surveys during my research – Peter McLeod, Terry Gill, Jim Culbert, P Finucane, Vincent McGee, Doris, Ann Talbot, Carol Harper, Sibyl Bahr, Jo McGarry, Sarah, Angela Costello, Louise Adams, Andrea Pettitt, Colleen Linehan, Barbara Collins, Jenny Duggan, T Maguire, Rebecca Enright, Joanne Condon, Maraget Gillhooley, Laura, Vicki Flores, Juncal, and Ruth Rooney, thank you all for your contributions. Thank you to these tweeters for helping me come up with typical farmer chatup lines @MrsButcherLimk, @Owenfitzp, @JoannMcCormish, @fluffanella, @NicowhaS and @YummyMummyby4.

To everyone who has read my blog irishfarmerette.com to date and especially to all those who commented on my blog post 'Advice to those considering marrying a farmer' which helped to persuade me there just might be a readership out there for my book. To Mairead, Liam, Corey and Donna – thank you all for spreading the word about my book on your blogs during the crowdfunding.

Acknowledgements

I would like to thank a number of good friends for your continued support. Paula Sheridan, Geraldine Walsh, Bianka McDonagh, Emma Geoghegan, Miriam Lloyd, Valerie Coleman, Teresa Keogh and Una Halpin of the Carlow CEB Think Tank for all your support and particularly all your shares during the crowdfunding campaign. Suzanna Crampton, Jo-Ann McCormish, Elaine Hall, Jo McGarry, Fionnuala Malone, Helena Fitzgerald, Hannah Bolger, Lily de Sylva, Imen McDonnell - all fellow farmerettes / farmhers. To Jane Steger-Lewis, thank you for rounding things up so often. Simon and Rozz Lewis, Beatrice Whelan, Maura Flynn, Marian Hearne, Damien Carroll, Valerie Humphreys, John O'Connor, Fiona Dillon, – all fellow KLCKers, thank you for your support. To Yukari Sweeney for being so lovely and optimistic every time we connect on social media.

Ruth Wildgust, Lisa McGee, Adrienne Walker, Diana Fahy, Jo Woods and Philippa Adams, thank you all for your long and valued friendships. Bernie Tracey, a wonderful mentor and friend, for always singing my praises and telling me the truth too. Marie Ennis O'Connor, Susan Dennehy and Dee Sewell for your continued friendship and support. Owen Fitzpatrick, my time management consultant, 'straight talking shrink' and good friend, thank you for all your support and for not telling me I was crazy. Madeleine Forrest, who goes to extraordinary lengths for all of her friends, thank you for being the most wonderful friend for so many years. Amanda Webb, my partner in crime in the Blog Awards and We Teach Social, thank you for your impulsiveness, wonderful advice, friendship and the supply of chocolates – you are marvellous.

To Sam, our wonderful cattle dog, who saves me from so much angst, running and shouting. You are worth your weight in gold.

To Brian, without whom there would not have been a book as after all, the inspiration hit me after a session of cattle sorting and "the BLACK one". You thought I was mad yet supported me every step of the way. You are the love of my life and here's to many more anniversaries.

To my wonderful children, Will and Kate, for making my heart sing every day. I love you to Pluto and back again.

[1] JB Keane, *The Field* (Mercier Press, 1991)

[2] *Irish Independent*, Rolling Back the Years Special Supplement, 3rd March 2012 pp4-7

[3] Sweeney, Frank, "It's the milkman", *History Ireland*, Jan/Feb 2010 Volume 18

[4] The Celtic Tiger was a building boom in Ireland from 2000-2008 which increased the value of property and the wealth of many.

[5] Stopping a gap means to help on the farm by preventing cattle or sheep going through an open gap or gateway.

[6] Gibbons, Mary, "Invisible Farmers – the role of Irish women in the National Farmers' Association, Farmers' Rights campaign of the 1960s", *Women and Gender Studies Series*, Volume 12 issue 1, September 2012

[7] ibid

[8] Ni Laoire, Caitríona, (2002) "Young farmers, masculinities and change in rural Ireland," *Irish Geography*, National University of Ireland, Maynooth p20.

[9] The marriage bar meant that women who married after 1st January 1933 had to give up work in civil service jobs. it was not lifted until 1973. Only 6% of married women were working in 1966.

[10] Macra na Feirme is an organisation open to farmers and non farmers until they reach 35. It is open to men and women who live in rural areas.

[11] Ni Laoire, pp6-27

[12] *Sunday Independent*, 18th April 1954

[13] Trevor, William, *The Ballroom of Romance and other stories* (Irish Independent, 2005)

[14] Connell, KH 1956

[15] Guinnane, Timothy, (1997) "The Vanishing Irish: Ireland's Population from the Great Famine to the Great War", *History Ireland*, Issue 2,

[16] Travers, Pauric, "'There was nothing for me there': Irish female emigration 1922-71" in *Irish Women and Irish*

Migration, edited by Patrick O'Sullivan (Leicester University Press, 1995) p149

[17] ibid, p151

[18] *Irish Independent*, 16th September 1940

[19] Travers, p42

[20] Daly Willie, *The Last Matchmaker*(2011)

[21] Luddy, Maria, *Women in Ireland 1800-1918: A Documentary History*, (Cork University Press, 1995) p30 (Taken from Michael MacDonagh, 'Marriage Customs in Rural Ireland', *The Englishwoman*, 22 (April – June 1914)

[22] *Anglo Celt*, 5th November 1955

[23] *The Last Matchmaker*

[24] *Irish Independent*, 4th March 1933 Marriage Dowry Claim, Verdict for Monaghan mother-in-law. Judge Sheehy dismissed a claim for £75 at Castleblaney Circuit court yesterday, brought by Peter Callan, Taplagh, against his mother-in-law Mrs Mary Hamill.

[25] *Irish Independent* 1st August 1984

[26] *The Last Matchmaker*

[27] Keane, JB, *Sive* (Mercier Press, 2009)

[28] Conrad Arensberg and Solon T. Kimball, *Family & community in Ireland*, Harvard, 1968

[29] *The Last Matchmaker*

[30] *Sive*

[31] *The Ballroom of Romance*

[32] Connell, KH,

[33] JB Keane, *Letters of a Love Hungry Farmer,* (Mercier Press, 2009)p46

[34] JB Keane, *The Chastitute* (Mercier Press, 1981)

[35] *Love Hungry Farmer*, p55

[36] Ibid, p47

[37] *Letters of a Matchmaker*

[38] Sayers, Peig, *An Old Woman's Reflections*, (Oxford Paperback, 1961)

[39] *Irish Press*, 16th October 1946

[40] *Letters of a Matchmaker*, p266

[41] *Sunday Independent*, 24th May 1959

[42] *The Ballroom of Romance*

[43] Eamonn De Valera was Taoiseach of Ireland from 1932-1948, 1951-1954 and 1957-1959 (Equivalent role to Prime Minister of Britain) He subsequently became President of Ireland.

[44] *The Irish Press*, 15th August 1956

[45] *Sunday Independent*, 24th May 1959

[46] *Irish Independent*, May 1960

[47] *Irish Independent*, 14th December 1955

[48] *Limerick Leader*, 29th May 1955

[49] *Irish Press*, 17th August 1971

[50] *Irish Press*, 19th January 1971

[51] Margo and Barbara are the wives in *The Good Life*, the BBC sitcom from the 1970s whereby Tom and Barbara Good attempt to live sustainably from their suburban house, living beside the initially disapproving Margo and Gerry.

[52] Road frontage refers to the fields that adjoin a road, preferably a main road, as it maximises their chance of getting planning permission and being sold as a site for a house. Instead of a value of €7-12,000 per acre, two acres sites were selling for over €200,000 during the Celtic Tiger.

[53] *The Good Life*, the BBC sitcom

[5454] *Letters of a Matchmaker*

[55] Interviews carried out as research (on telephone and in an online survey).

[56] *The Ballroom of Romance*, p47

[57] Macra na Feirme

[58] The Muddy Matches online dating site caters for rural dwellers in Ireland and the UK

[59] A "liquid milk" contract means that the farmer is contracted to provide milk that will be sold as fresh milk in shops hence they have to provide milk 365 days of the year. Manufacturing milk is used to make cheese, butter, yoghurt, infant formula and milk is provided for approximately ten months of the year.

[60] Monahan, Oonagh, *Money for Jam,* (Oak Tree Press, 2013) for direction on starting a small food business.

[61] Murphy, Catriona, "The fear that stalks our farms," *Irish Independent,* 21, 23 & 24 January 2012 – An excellent and award-winning series of articles on pre-nuptial agreements for farming families.

[62] *Irish Independent* 9th November 1995

[63] Murphy, Caitriona, "Why farm couples should take a lesson from Kim and Kanye" *Irish Independent* 4 November 2012

[64] *Agriland.ie* "Calls for Legal Clarity", 31 October 2013

[65] Murphy, "The fear that stalks our farms" *Irish Independent* 21, 23 &24 January 2012

[66] *Irish Independent,* 20 Jan 2009

[67] Irishcentral.com - James O'Shea *"Top ten reasons why Irish people file a divorce or so they say"* 21 August 2013

[68] Women and Agriculture conference, 2009

[69] *Letters of a Matchmaker,* p266

[70] According to a Macra na Feirme survey 2013

[71] Infections such as Chlyamydophila abortus, toxoplasma or listeria can cause severe illness to a pregnant woman and death or deformity to the growing baby.